Ultimate 4 Ingredient Cookbook

Meals in Minutes

Cookbook Resources, LLC
Highland Village, Texas

Ultimate 4 Ingredient Cookbook
Meals in Minutes

1st Printing - April 2010

International Standard Book Number: 978-1-59769-016-4

Library of Congress Control Number: 2010012849

Library of Congress Cataloging-in-Publication Data

    Ultimate 4 ingredient cookbook : meals in minutes.
      p. cm.
    Includes index.
    ISBN 978-1-59769-016-4
    1. Quick and easy cookery. I. Cookbook Resources, LLC. II. Title.
    TX833.5.U45 2010
    641.5'55--dc22

                      2010012849

Cover and Illustration by Nancy Bohanan

Edited, Designed, Published and Manufactured in the United States of America by
Cookbook Resources, LLC
541 Doubletree Drive
Highland Village, Texas 75077

Toll free 866-229-2665

www.cookbookresources.com

Bringing Family and Friends to the Table

Family Meals in Minutes!

In our fast-paced, rush-here-and-there lives, a home-cooked meal may be considered a luxury. We live out of our cars, placing food orders on cell phones and going to drive-through windows for the night's meal — and maybe the family sits down together to eat.

We want to help families come back to the table and spend quality time together while sharing good food. The recipes in *Ultimate 4 Ingredient Cookbook* are easy to prepare and the ingredients are readily available. Most of them are already in your pantry.

Everyone in the family can cook out of *Ultimate 4 Ingredient Cookbook*. Mouth-watering meals are just minutes away and every minute we spend around the table enriches our lives and helps us grow stronger.

Please enjoy and don't hesitate to recruit some helpers!

More statistical studies are finding that family meals play a significant role in childhood development. Children who eat with their families four or more nights per week are healthier, make better grades in school, score higher on aptitude tests and are less likely to have problems with drugs.

Contents

This icon indicates a microwave recipe.

Appetizers

Chicky Cheese Spread

2 (8 ounce) packages cream cheese, softened
2 tablespoons marinade for chicken
2 cups cooked, finely shredded chicken breasts
¼ cup chopped almonds, toasted

- Beat cream cheese and marinade for chicken in bowl until creamy.

- Fold in shredded chicken and almonds. Yields 1½ pints.

*TIP: One way to use this spread is to spread on English muffin halves
and toast, but be careful not to brown.*

Spicy Beef and Cheese Dip

1 (10 ounce) can diced tomatoes and green chilies
½ teaspoon garlic powder
2 (16 ounce) packages cubed Velveeta® cheese
1 pound lean ground beef, cooked, drained

- Combine tomatoes and green chilies, garlic powder, and cheese
in large saucepan.

- Heat on low and stir constantly until cheese melts. Add ground
beef and mix well. Yields 3 cups.

*Green chiles provide more vitamin C
than any other vegetable and twice as
much as citrus fruits. As they ripen
and turn red, vitamin C decreases and
vitamin A increases.*

Chippy Beef Dip

1 (8 ounce) package cream cheese, softened
1 (8 ounce) carton sour cream
1 (2.5 ounce) jar sliced dried beef, cubed
½ cup finely chopped pecans

- Beat cream cheese and sour cream in bowl until creamy.

- Fold in dried beef and pecans. Refrigerate. Yields 1 pint.

Artichoke-Bacon Dip

1 (14 ounce) jar marinated artichoke hearts, drained, chopped
1 cup mayonnaise
2 teaspoons Worcestershire sauce
5 slices bacon, cooked crisp, crumbled

- Preheat oven to 350°.

- Combine all ingredients in large bowl. Pour into sprayed 8-inch baking dish.

- Bake for 12 minutes. Yields 1½ cups.

Spicy Ham Dip

2 (8 ounce) packages cream cheese, softened
2 (6 ounce) cans deviled ham
1 heaping tablespoon horseradish
¼ cup minced onion

- Beat cream cheese in bowl until creamy.

- Add remaining ingredients. Refrigerate. Yields 1½ pints.

Dippy Ham Spread

1 (5 ounce) jar pimento cheese spread
1 (4 ounce) can deviled ham
1 cup mayonnaise
1 bunch fresh green onions, chopped

- Combine, cheese spread, ham and mayonnaise in medium bowl and mix until they blend well.

- Fold in chopped green onions. Yields 1 pint.

Chunky Shrimp Dip

2 (6 ounce) cans shrimp, drained
2 cups mayonnaise
6 green onions, finely chopped
¾ cup chunky salsa

- Crumble shrimp and stir in mayonnaise, onion and salsa in bowl.

- Refrigerate for 1 to 2 hours. Yields 1½ pints.

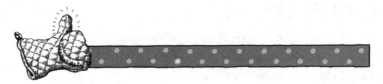

Do what you can, with what you have, where you are. Theodore Roosevelt

Party Shrimp Dip

1 (8 ounce) package cream cheese, softened
½ cup mayonnaise
1 (6 ounce) can tiny, cooked shrimp, drained
¾ teaspoon Creole seasoning

- Beat cream cheese and mayonnaise in bowl. Stir in shrimp and seasoning.

- Mix well and refrigerate. Yields 1 pint.

Quickie Shrimp Dunk

1 (8 ounce) package cream cheese, softened
1 cup cocktail sauce
1 teaspoon Italian herb seasoning
1 (6 ounce) can tiny shrimp, drained

- Beat cream cheese in bowl until smooth.

- Add remaining ingredients and refrigerate. Yields 1 pint.

Easy Tuna Dip

1 (6 ounce) can tuna, drained
1 (1 ounce) packet Italian salad dressing mix
1 (8 ounce) carton sour cream
2 green onions with tops, chopped

- Combine all ingredients in bowl and mix well. Refrigerate for several hours before serving. Yields 1½ cups.

Tuna Melt Snack

1 (10 ounce) package frozen spinach, drained
2 (6 ounce) cans white tuna in water, drained, flaked
¾ cup mayonnaise
1½ cups shredded mozzarella cheese, divided

- Preheat oven to 350°.

- Squeeze spinach between paper towels to completely remove excess moisture.

- Combine spinach, tuna, mayonnaise and 1 cup cheese in large bowl and mix well.

- Spoon into sprayed pie pan and bake for 15 minutes.

- Remove from oven and sprinkle remaining cheese over top. Bake for additional 5 minutes. Yields 1½ pints.

Cheesy Crab Dip

1 (6 ounce) roll garlic cheese, diced
1 (10 ounce) can cream of mushroom soup
1 (6 ounce) can crabmeat, drained, flaked
2 tablespoons sherry

- Heat all ingredients in medium saucepan and stir until cheese melts.

- Keep warm in chafing dish. Yields 1 pint.

Crab Quackers

1 (6 ounce) can crabmeat, drained, flaked
1 (8 ounce) package cream cheese, softened
2 (10 ounce) cans cream of celery soup
1 (4 ounce) can chopped black olives

- Combine all ingredients in saucepan and stir constantly until cheese melts. Yields 1½ pints.

Unbelievable Crab Dip

1 (6 ounce) can white crabmeat, drained, flaked
1 (8 ounce) package cream cheese
½ cup (1 stick) butter

- Combine crabmeat, cream cheese and butter in saucepan.

- Heat, stir constantly until thoroughly mixed. Transfer to chafing dish. Yields 1½ cups.

Fast Clam Dip

1 (1 ounce) packet onion soup mix
1 (16 ounce) carton sour cream
1 (7 ounce) can minced clams, drained
2 tablespoons chili sauce

- Combine onion soup mix and sour cream in bowl and mix well.

- Add clams and chili sauce. Mix well and refrigerate. Yields 1 pint.

Snappy Clam Dunk

1½ (8 ounce) packages cream cheese
¼ cup (½ stick) butter
2 (6 ounce) cans minced clams, drained
½ teaspoon Worcestershire sauce

- Melt cream cheese and butter in double boiler. Add clams and Worcestershire sauce. Serve hot. Yields 1 pint.

Pepper Pot-Bean Dip

1 (15 ounce) can refried beans
1 (16 ounce) package cubed Mexican Velveeta® cheese
½ cup (1 stick) butter
1 teaspoon garlic powder

- Combine all ingredients in large double boiler. Heat on low, stirring often, until cheese and butter melt.

- Serve hot in chafing dish. Yields 1½ pints.

Speedy Gonzales

1 (16 ounce) package cubed Velveeta° cheese
½ cup milk
1 (12 ounce) jar salsa, divided
Tortilla chips

- Melt cheese and milk in double boiler.

- Add about half salsa. Serve with tortilla chips. Yields 1½ pints.

TIP: Add more salsa for extra heat.

Speedy Cheese Dip

2 (10 ounce) cans cheddar cheese soup
1 (10 ounce) can diced tomatoes and green chilies
1 (10 ounce) can cream of chicken soup
Pinch of cayenne pepper

- Mix all ingredients in saucepan.

- Serve hot with chips. Yields 2½ cups.

Smoky Gouda Spread

¾ cup chopped walnuts
1 (8 ounce) smoked gouda cheese, softened
1 (8 ounce) package cream cheese, softened
¼ cup sliced green onions

- Preheat oven to 325°.

- Spread walnuts in shallow baking pan. Bake for 10 minutes or until lightly toasted. Cool and set aside.

- Trim and discard outer red edge of gouda cheese. Beat cream cheese and gouda cheese in bowl. Mix well and stir in walnuts and onions. Yields 1 pint.

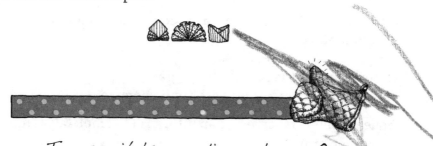

Two cannibals are eating a clown. One says to the other, "Does this taste funny to you?"

Amaretto Dip Spread

1 (8 ounce) package cream cheese, softened
¼ cup amaretto liqueur
¼ cup chopped slivered almonds, toasted

- Beat cream cheese and amaretto in bowl. Stir in toasted almonds. Yields 1 cup.

TIP: This is also a good spread on banana bread, zucchini bread, etc.

Black Olive Spread

1 (8 ounce) package cream cheese, softened
½ cup mayonnaise
1 (4 ounce) can chopped black olives, drained
3 fresh green onions, chopped very fine

- Beat cream cheese and mayonnaise in bowl until smooth.

- Add olives and onions and refrigerate. Yields 1 pint.

Simple Veggie Dip

1 (10 ounce) package frozen, chopped spinach, thawed,
   well drained
1 (16 ounce) carton sour cream
1 (1 ounce) packet vegetable soup mix
1 bunch fresh green onions with tops, chopped

- Squeeze spinach between paper towels to completely remove excess moisture.

- Combine all ingredients in glass bowl. Refrigerate for several hours before serving. Yields 1½ pints.

Tangy Artichoke Mix

½ cup (1 stick) butter
1 (14 ounce) can artichoke hearts, drained, chopped
1 (4 ounce) carton crumbled blue cheese
2 teaspoons lemon juice

- Melt butter in skillet and mix in artichoke hearts.

- Add blue cheese and lemon juice. Serve hot. Yields 1½ cups.

Italiano Artichoke Spread

1 (14 ounce) can artichoke hearts, drained, finely chopped
1 cup mayonnaise
1 cup grated parmesan cheese
1 (1 ounce) packet Italian salad dressing mix

- Preheat oven to 350°.

- Remove tough outer leaves and chop artichoke hearts.
  Combine all ingredients in bowl and mix thoroughly.

- Pour into 8-inch square baking pan. Bake for 20 minutes.
  Yields 1½ pints.

Avocado Olé

3 large ripe avocados, mashed
1 tablespoon fresh lemon juice
1 (1 ounce) packet onion soup mix
1 (8 ounce) carton sour cream

- Mix avocados with lemon juice in bowl and blend in soup mix
  and sour cream. Yields 1 pint.

Holy Guacamole

4 avocados, peeled
½ cup salsa
¼ cup sour cream
Tortilla chips

- Split avocados and remove seeds. Mash avocado with fork in bowl.

- Add salsa and sour cream. Serve with tortilla chips. Yields 1 pint.

Broccoli-Cheese Dip

1 (10 ounce) can broccoli-cheese soup
1 (10 ounce) package frozen, chopped broccoli, thawed
½ cup sour cream
2 teaspoons of dijon-style mustard

- Combine soup, broccoli, sour cream and mustard in saucepan and mix well.

- Heat and serve hot. Yields 1½ pints.

Confetti Dip

1 (15 ounce) can whole kernel corn, drained
1 (15 ounce) can black beans, drained
⅓ cup Italian salad dressing
1 (16 ounce) jar salsa

- Combine all ingredients in bowl.

- Refrigerate for several hours before serving. Yields 1 quart.

Creamy Cheesy Broccoli Dip

1 (10 ounce) package frozen, chopped broccoli, thawed, drained
1 (10 ounce) can cream of chicken soup
3 cups shredded cheddar cheese
1 (7 ounce) can diced green chilies

- Cook broccoli according to package directions in saucepan.

- Add soup, cheese and green chilies.

- Heat and stir constantly until cheese melts. Yields 1 pint.

Creamy Cucumber Spread

1 cup peeled, seeded, chopped cucumbers
1 (8 ounce) package cream cheese, softened
½ cup mayonnaise
1 teaspoon salt

- Before chopping cucumber, remove seeds.

- Beat cream cheese in bowl until creamy. Add mayonnaise, salt and cucumber. Yields 1 pint.

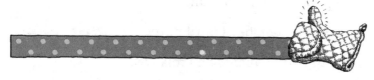

The most authentic guacamole is made by mashing very ripe avocados with a fork, which makes it lumpy with chunks of avocado. Processing avocado in a blender will not give the same texture. Chiles, fresh cilantro, fresh garlic, onion, tomato, and lemon or lime juice are all acceptable ingredients for the traditional guacamole.

Cucumber-Garlic Garden

2 cucumbers with peels
2 (8 ounce) packages cream cheese, softened
2 tablespoons lemon juice
1 (1 ounce) packet savory herb and garlic onion soup mix

- Coarsely grate both cucumbers and set aside liquid.

- Beat cream cheese, lemon juice and onion soup mix in bowl. Beat until cream cheese is fairly smooth.

- Thin mixture with set aside cucumber liquid as needed. Cover and refrigerate. Yields 1½ pints.

TIP: *Instead of using crackers or chips with this dip, try vegetables like carrots, celery, green onions, cauliflower and/or broccoli.*

Sassy Onion Dip

1 (8 ounce) package cream cheese, softened
1 (8 ounce) carton sour cream
½ cup chili sauce
1 (1 ounce) packet onion soup mix

- Beat cream cheese in bowl until fluffy.

- Add remaining ingredients and mix well.

- Cover and refrigerate. Yields 1½ cups.

If nothing is going well, call your grandmother. Italian Proverb

Spinach-Artichoke Dip

2 (10 ounce) boxes frozen spinach, thawed, drained
1 (14 ounce) jar marinated artichoke hearts, drained,
    finely chopped
1 cup mayonnaise
1 (8 ounce) package shredded mozzarella cheese

- Squeeze spinach between paper towels to remove excess moisture.

- Combine spinach, artichoke hearts, mayonnaise and cheese in bowl and mix well.

- Cover and refrigerate. Yields 1 quart.

Talking Tomato Dip

1 (10 ounce) can diced tomatoes and green chilies, drained
1 (8 ounce) carton sour cream
2 teaspoons horseradish

- Combine all ingredients in bowl. Refrigerate. Yields 1 pint.

Eggxcellent Dip

5 eggs, hard-boiled, mashed
1 cup mayonnaise
½ cup shredded Monterey Jack cheese
½ teaspoon mustard

- Combine all ingredients in bowl and mix well.

- Refrigerate for 1 hour before serving. Yields 1½ cups.

Breezy Pineapple-Island Spread

2 (8 ounce) packages cream cheese, softened
1 (8 ounce) carton sour cream
1 (8 ounce) can crushed pineapple, drained
½ cup finely chopped pecans

- Beat cream cheese and sour cream in bowl until creamy.

- Fold in pineapple and pecans and mix well. Refrigerate.
  Yields 1½ pints.

Nutty Apple Dip

1 (8 ounce) package cream cheese, softened
1 cup packed brown sugar
1 teaspoon vanilla
1 cup finely chopped pecans

- Beat cream cheese, sugar and vanilla in bowl until smooth.

- Stir in pecans. Yields 1 pint.

Crunchy Orange Dip for Apples

1 (8 ounce) package cream cheese, softened
1 (8 ounce) carton orange yogurt
½ cup orange marmalade
¼ cup finely chopped pecans

- Beat cream cheese in bowl until smooth.

- Fold in remaining ingredients and refrigerate. Yields 1 pint.

Creamy Orange Dip

1 (6 ounce) can frozen orange juice concentrate, thawed
1 (3.4 ounce) package vanilla instant pudding mix
1 cup milk
¼ cup sour cream

- Combine orange juice concentrate, vanilla pudding mix and milk in bowl. Stir with whisk until mixture blends and is smooth. Stir in sour cream.

- Cover and refrigerate for at least 2 hours. Yields 1 pint.

Chocolate Fruit Dip

1 (8 ounce) package cream cheese, softened
¼ cup chocolate syrup
1 (7 ounce) jar marshmallow creme
Fresh fruit

- Beat cream cheese and chocolate syrup in bowl until smooth.

- Fold in marshmallow creme.

- Cover and refrigerate until serving. Yields 1 pint.

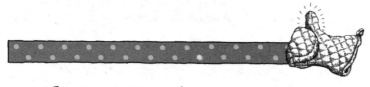

Those who have been intoxicated with power... can never willingly abandon it.
Edmund Burke

Beefy Cheese Round

2 (8 ounce) packages cream cheese, softened
2 (2.5 ounce) jars dried beef
1 bunch fresh green onions with tops, chopped
1 teaspoon cayenne pepper

- Beat cream cheese in bowl until smooth and creamy.

- Chop dried beef in food processor or blender.

- Combine cream cheese, beef, onions and cayenne pepper.

- Form into ball and refrigerate overnight. Yields 1½ pints.

Quick-and-Easy Sausage Balls

1 pound hot pork sausage
1 (16 ounce) package shredded cheddar cheese
3 cups biscuit mix
⅓ cup milk

- Preheat oven to 375°.

- Combine all ingredients in bowl and form into small balls. If dough is a little too sticky, add 1 teaspoon more biscuit mix.

- Bake for 13 to 15 minutes. Yields 20 to 28 balls.

To make bell pepper strips or slices, hold the pepper upright on a cutting surface. Slice each of the sides from the pepper stem and discard stem, white membrane and seeds.

Great Balls of Fire

1 pound lean hot sausage
3 green onions, chopped
1 (10 ounce) can diced tomatoes and green chilies
2 (16 ounce) packages cubed Velveeta® cheese

- Brown sausage and onion in large skillet. Drain fat.

- Add tomatoes and green chilies and mix.

- Add cheese to sausage mixture and cook on low heat until cheese melts. Serve hot in chafing dish. Yields 1 quart.

Sausage Pinwheels

1 (1 pound) package hot sausage
2½ cups biscuit mix
⅔ cup milk
1 green or red bell pepper, minced

- Let sausage come to room temperature.

- Combine biscuit mix and milk in medium bowl and mix well.

- Divide dough into 3 parts. Roll each piece of dough into thin rectangle.

- Crumble one-third sausage and minced bell pepper on each piece of dough and pat down. Roll like jellyroll, cover with foil and refrigerate overnight.

- When ready to bake, preheat oven to 375°.

- Slice into thin slices and bake for 15 to 20 minutes. Yields 20 to 30.

Sausage Bites

1 (1 pound) package hot sausage
1 (16 ounce) package shredded colby or cheddar cheese
3¾ cups biscuit mix
½ teaspoon garlic powder

- Preheat oven to 350°.

- Combine sausage, cheese, biscuit mix and garlic powder in bowl. Knead thoroughly.

- Roll into 1-inch balls.

- Bake on baking sheet for 15 to 18 minutes or until light brown. Yields 24 to 30.

Crispy Chestnuts

1 (8 ounce) can whole water chestnuts, drained
5 - 6 slices bacon, quartered
Honey-mustard salad dressing

- Wrap each water chestnut with strip of bacon. Secure with toothpick.

- Broil until bacon cooks. Dip in honey-mustard. Yields 20 to 24.

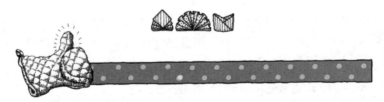

Garlic salt and garlic powder will last up to one year. To avoid sodium, it is better to use garlic powder rather than garlic salt.

Bacon Nibblers

1 (2 pound) package sliced bacon
1½ cups packed brown sugar
1½ teaspoons dry mustard
¼ teaspoon pepper

- Preheat oven to 325º.

- Let bacon come to room temperature. Cut each slice in half.

- Combine brown sugar, dry mustard and pepper in shallow bowl.

- Dip each half slice bacon in brown sugar mixture and press down so bacon coats well. Place each slice on baking sheet with sides.

- Bake for 25 minutes, turning once, until bacon browns. Immediately remove with tongs to several layers of paper towels. Bacon will harden and can be broken in pieces. Yields 40.

Bacon-Wrapped Water Chestnuts

1 (8 ounce) can whole water chestnuts, drained
¼ cup soy sauce
¼ - ¾ teaspoon cayenne pepper
About ½ pound bacon, cut in thirds

- Marinate water chestnuts for 1 hour in soy sauce and cayenne pepper.

- Wrap one-third slice bacon around each water chestnut and fasten with toothpick.

- When ready to bake, preheat oven to 375º.

- Bake for 20 minutes or until bacon is done. Drain and serve hot. Yields 15 to 18.

Ranch Round-Up

1 (1 ounce) packet ranch-style salad dressing mix
2 (8 ounce) packages cream cheese, softened
¼ cup finely chopped pecans
1 (3 ounce) jar real bacon bits

- Beat dressing mix and cream cheese in bowl.

- Roll into ball. Roll cheese ball in pecans and bacon bits.

- Refrigerate for several hours before serving. Yields 1 pint.

English Muffin Pizzas

English muffins, halved
Canned or bottled pizza sauce
Sliced salami or pepperoni
Shredded mozzarella or cheddar cheese

- Split muffins in half. Spread muffin with canned pizza sauce.

- Add salami or pepperoni.

- Top with cheese and place under broiler until cheese melts and begins to bubble.

TIP: *If you want to go all out, add some or all of the following ingredients: cooked chopped onion, cooked chopped bell pepper, sliced jalapeno peppers and chopped green or black olives.*

A grandmother pretends she doesn't know who you are on Halloween. Erma Bombeck

Peppy Frank Bits

1 (8 count) package frankfurters
1 (8 ounce) package cornbread muffin mix
½ teaspoon chili powder
⅔ cup milk

- Cut franks into 1-inch pieces.

- Combine corn muffin mix, chili powder and milk in bowl. Add frankfurter pieces to corn muffin mix and stir well to coat each piece.

- Drop one at a time into hot oil in deep fryer. Fry for 2 minutes or until brown, then drain. Yields 24 to 32.

TIP: Serve warm with chili sauce for dunking.

Bubbly Fast Franks

1 (10 count) package wieners
½ cup chili sauce
½ cup packed brown sugar
½ cup bourbon

- Cut wieners into bite-size pieces.

- Combine chili sauce, brown sugar and bourbon in saucepan.

- Add wieners to sauce and simmer for 30 minutes. Serve in chafing dish. Yields 1 pint.

Crispy Crab

¾ cup shredded cheddar cheese
½ cup (1 stick) butter, softened
1 (6 ounce) can crabmeat, drained, flaked
4 English muffins, halved

- Combine cheese, butter and crabmeat in bowl and mix well.

- Spread mixture on each muffin half. Cut each muffin into quarters and place on baking sheet.

- Broil for 5 minutes and serve hot. Yields 32.

Shrimp Squares Deluxe

1 (6 ounce) can shrimp, drained, chopped
1 cup mayonnaise
1 cup shredded cheddar cheese
10-12 slices white bread, trimmed, cut in squares

- Combine shrimp, mayonnaise and cheese in bowl.

- Spread shrimp mixture on bread squares and broil until bubbly. Yields 40 to 48 squares.

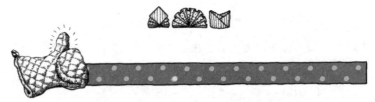

California produces 99% of the nation's agricultural crops for almonds, artichokes, clingstone peaches, dried plums, figs, olives, persimmons, pomegranates, raisins, ladino clover seed, sweet rice and walnuts.

Quickie Bacon-Oyster Bites

1 (5 ounce) can smoked oysters, drained, chopped
⅔ cup herb-seasoned stuffing mix
8 slices bacon, halved, partially cooked

- Preheat oven to 350°.

- Combine oysters, stuffing mix and ¼ cup water in bowl. Add 1 teaspoon water if mixture seems too dry.

- Form into balls and use 1 tablespoon mixture for each.

- Wrap ½ slice bacon around each and secure with toothpick.

- Place on rack in shallow baking pan. Cook for 25 to 30 minutes. Yields 16 bites.

Artichoke Bites

1½ cups mayonnaise
¾ cup freshly grated parmesan cheese
1 (4 ounce) can diced green chilies
1 (14 ounce) jar artichoke hearts, drained, chopped

- Mix mayonnaise, parmesan cheese, green chilies and artichoke hearts in bowl. Yields 1½ pints.

Why do you put bells on cows
Because the horns don't work.

Summertime Cucumber Spread

1 (8 ounce) package cream cheese, softened
½ teaspoon dill weed
3 medium cucumbers, peeled, grated, drained
1 (1 ounce) packet ranch salad dressing mix

- Beat cream cheese and dill weed in bowl until creamy.

- Fold in cucumbers and ranch dressing. Yields 1 pint.

Onion Crisps

1 cup (2 sticks) butter, softened
1 (8 ounce) package shredded cheddar cheese
1 (1 ounce) packet onion soup mix
2 cups flour

- Combine all ingredients in bowl. Dough will be very thick.

- Divide into 2 batches and form into 2 rolls. Refrigerate for about 3 hours.

- When ready to bake, preheat oven to 350º.

- Cut in ¼-thick slices. Bake for 12 to 15 minutes. Yields 30 to 40.

*Friendship consists in forgetting
what one gives and remembering what
one receives.*

Chili-Cheese Balls

1 (8 ounce) package shredded sharp cheddar cheese, softened
½ cup (1 stick) butter, softened
1 cup flour
1 (4 ounce) can diced green chilies

- Preheat oven to 375°.

- Mix cheese and butter in bowl. Add flour and green chilies.

- Form dough into 2-inch balls and place on baking sheet. Bake for 14 to 15 minutes. Yields 12 to 16 balls.

Blue Cheese Ball

3 fresh green onions with tops
1 (8 ounce) and 1 (3 ounce) package cream cheese, softened
1 (4 ounce) package crumbled blue cheese
⅓ cup finely chopped pecans

- Finely chop white portion of onions, combine with cream cheese and blue cheese in bowl and beat well. Shape into ball.

- Finely chop green tops of onions and combine with pecans. Roll cheese ball in mixture to cover completely.

- Refrigerate for at least 3 hours. Yields 1 pint.

Research shows that chiles can boost your metabolism rate, causing your body to burn calories faster.

Cheddar Cheese Ring

2 (16 ounce) packages shredded cheddar cheese
1 small onion, finely chopped
1 cup mayonnaise
1½ cups plus 2 tablespoons finely chopped pecans

- Combine cheese, onion, mayonnaise and 1½ cups pecans in bowl. Press into 8-inch ring mold.

- Cover with plastic wrap and refrigerate until set. Remove from mold when firm.

- Sprinkle top of cheese ring with remaining pecans.

- Slice to serve. Yields 1½ pints.

EZ Cheese Straws

1 (5 ounce) box piecrust mix
¾ cup shredded cheddar cheese
Cayenne pepper
¼ teaspoon garlic powder

- Preheat oven to 350°.

- Prepare piecrust according to package directions. Roll into rectangular shape.

- Sprinkle cheese over dough and press cheese into dough.

- Sprinkle cayenne pepper over cheese.

- Fold dough over once to cover cheese. Roll to make ¼-inch thickness.

- Cut dough into ½ x 3-inch strips and place on lightly sprayed baking sheet.

- Bake for 12 to 15 minutes. Yields 20 to 25.

Snappy Olive-Cheese Appetizers

1 cup chopped pimento-stuffed olives
2 fresh green onions, finely chopped
1½ cups shredded Monterey Jack cheese
½ cup mayonnaise

- Preheat oven to 375°.

- Combine all ingredients in large bowl and mix well. Yields
  1 pint.

TIP: *Spread on English muffins and bake until bubbly. Cut muffins
into quarters and serve hot.*

Tortilla Rollers

1 (8 ounce) package cream cheese, softened
1 (4 ounce) can chopped black olives, drained
1 (12 ounce) jar salsa, divided
Flour tortillas

- Beat cream cheese in bowl until smooth. Add black olives and
  ¼ cup salsa and mix well.

- To serve, spread on flour tortillas and roll. Refrigerate for
  several hours.

- Slice in ½-inch slices. Insert toothpick in each slice and dip in
  remaining salsa. Yields 1 pint.

Easy Toasted Pecans

12 cups pecan halves
½ cup (1 stick) butter
1 tablespoon salt
1 tablespoon garlic powder

- Preheat oven to 250°.

- Place pecans in large baking pan and toast for 15 minutes to dry.

- Slice butter and melt in baking pan. Add pecans and stir to coat completely.

- After pecans and butter mix well, sprinkle with salt and garlic powder and stir often.

- Toast pecans for 1 hour or until butter absorbs and pecans are crisp. Yields 3 quarts.

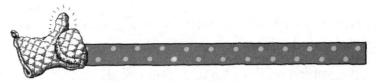

"Doc, I can't stop singing 'The Green Green Grass of Home.'"

"That sounds like Tom Jones Syndrome."

"Is it common?"

"Well, it's not unusual."

Beverages

Shady Lady's Apricot Punch

1 (12 ounce) can apricot nectar, chilled
1 (6 ounce) can frozen orange juice concentrate, thawed
2 tablespoons lemon juice
1 (2 liter) bottle ginger ale, chilled

- Combine apricot nectar, orange juice concentrate, lemon juice and 1 cup water. Refrigerate.

- When ready to serve, stir in ginger ale. Yields 3 quarts.

Best Tropical Punch

1 (46 ounce) can pineapple juice
1 (46 ounce) can apricot nectar
3 (6 ounce) cans frozen limeade concentrate, thawed
3 quarts ginger ale, chilled

- Combine pineapple juice, apricot nectar and limeade in container and refrigerate.

- When ready to serve, add ginger ale. Yields 1½ gallons.

South Seas Cranberry Punch

2 (28 ounce) bottles ginger ale, chilled
1 (48 ounce) can pineapple juice, chilled
1 quart cranberry juice, chilled
1 quart pineapple sherbet, broken up

- Pour all ingredients in punch bowl. Serve immediately. Yields 1½ gallons.

Perfect Party Punch

1 (12 ounce) can frozen limeade concentrate
1 (46 ounce) can pineapple juice, chilled
1 (46 ounce) apricot nectar, chilled
1 quart ginger ale, chilled

- Dilute limeade concentrate according to can directions.

- Add pineapple juice and apricot nectar and stir well.

- When ready to serve, add ginger ale. Yields 1½ gallons.

Creamy Strawberry Punch

1 (10 ounce) package frozen strawberries, thawed
½ gallon strawberry ice cream, softened
2 (2 liter) bottles ginger ale, chilled
Fresh strawberries

- Process frozen strawberries through blender.

- Combine strawberries, chunks of ice cream and ginger ale in punch bowl.

- Stir and serve immediately. Garnish with fresh strawberries. Yields 1 gallon.

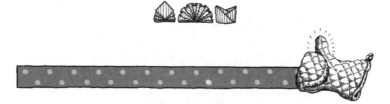

The reason grandchildren and grandparents get along so well is that they have a common enemy. Sam Levenson

Strawberry Fizz Whiz

2 (10 ounce) boxes frozen strawberries, thawed
2 (6 ounce) cans frozen pink lemonade concentrate
2 (2 liter) bottles ginger ale, chilled
Fresh strawberries

- Process strawberries through blender.

- Pour lemonade into punch bowl and stir in processed strawberries.

- Add chilled ginger ale and stir well. Garnish with fresh strawberries. Yields 3 quarts.

TIP: It would be nice to make an ice ring out of another bottle of ginger ale.

Party Hardy Punch

1 (46 ounce) can pineapple juice
1 (46 ounce) can apple juice
3 quarts ginger ale, chilled
Pineapple chunks

- Combine pineapple and apple juice in 2 large plastic containers. Freeze both juices.

- When ready to serve, place frozen pineapple and apple juices in punch bowl and add chilled ginger ale.

- Stir to mix. Garnish with pineapple chunks. Yields 1½ gallons.

Pina Colada Punch

1 (46 ounce) can pineapple juice, chilled
1 (20 ounce) can crushed pineapple with liquid
1 (15 ounce) can cream of coconut
1 (32 ounce) bottle lemon-lime carbonated drink, chilled

- Combine all ingredients in punch bowl.

- Serve over ice cubes. Yields 1 gallon.

Victorian Iced Tea

4 individual tea bags
¼ cup sugar
1 (12 ounce) can frozen cranberry-raspberry juice
    concentrate, thawed

- Place tea bags in teapot and add 4 cups boiling water. Cover and
  steep for 5 minutes.

- Remove and discard tea bags. Add sugar and mix. Refrigerate.

- Just before serving, combine cranberry-raspberry concentrate
  and cold water according to concentrate directions in 2½-quart
  pitcher.

- Stir in tea and serve with ice cubes. Yields 2½ quarts.

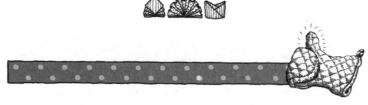

In time of test, family is best.
Burmese Proverb

Sparkling Wine Punch

6 oranges with peels, thinly sliced
1 cup sugar
2 (750 ml) bottles dry white wine
3 (750 ml) bottles sparkling wine, chilled

- Place orange slices in large plastic or glass container and sprinkle with sugar.

- Add white wine, cover and refrigerate for at least 8 hours.

- Stir in sparkling wine. Yields 1 gallon.

Champagne Punch

1 (750 ml) bottle champagne, chilled
1 (32 ounce) bottle ginger ale, chilled
1 (6 ounce) can frozen orange juice concentrate
Orange slices

- Mix champagne, ginger ale and orange juice in punch bowl.

- Refrigerate and serve. Garnish with orange slices. Yields 1½ quarts.

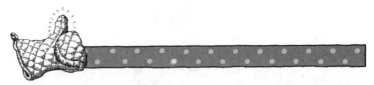

A jumper cable walks into a bar and sits down. The bartender says, "Okay, I'll serve you, but don't start anything."

Apple Party Punch

3 cups sparkling apple cider
2 cups apple juice
1 cup pineapple juice
½ cup brandy

- Combine all ingredients in container and freeze for 8 hours.

- Remove punch from freezer 30 minutes before serving.

- Place in small punch bowl and break into chunks. Stir until slushy. Yields 1½ quarts.

Amaretto Cooler

1¼ cups amaretto liqueur
2 quarts orange juice
1 (15 ounce) bottle club soda, chilled
Orange slices

- Combine amaretto, orange juice and club soda in container and stir well.

- Serve over ice. Garnish with orange slices. Yields 2½ quarts.

Fuji apples came to the American market in the 1980's from Japan. Today, more Fuji apples are grown in the U.S. than in Japan. They are known for their crisp sweetness and beautiful reddish-pink color.

Sparkling Pink Party

3 (6 ounce) cans frozen pink lemonade concentrate
1 (750 ml) bottle pink sparkling wine
3 (2 liter) bottles lemon-lime carbonated beverage, divided
Lime slices

- Combine pink lemonade, sparkling wine and 1 bottle carbonated beverage in airtight container, cover and freeze for 8 hours or until firm.

- Let stand at room temperature 10 minutes and place in punch bowl.

- Add remaining bottle carbonated beverage and stir until slushy. Garnish with lime slices. Yields 3 quarts.

Holiday Eggnog

1 gallon eggnog
1 (1 pint) carton whipping cream
1 quart brandy
½ gallon vanilla ice cream, softened

- Mix all ingredients in bowl.

- Pour into individual cups and serve immediately. Yields 1½ gallons.

TIP: *Sprinkle with nutmeg for a nice touch.*

Lemonade Tea

2 family-size tea bags
½ cup sugar
1 (12 ounce) can frozen lemonade concentrate
1 quart ginger ale, chilled

- Steep tea in 3 quarts water in container and mix with sugar and lemonade.

- Add ginger ale just before serving. Yields 1 gallon.

Hot Cranberry Cider

1½ quarts cranberry juice
1 (12 ounce) can frozen orange juice concentrate, thawed
½ teaspoon ground cinnamon
Sugar, optional

- Combine cranberry juice, orange juice and 1½ orange juice cans water in large saucepan. Bring to a boil to blend flavors.

- Add cinnamon and stir well. Add sugar if needed. Serve hot. Yields 2 quarts.

TIP: Orange slices make a nice garnish.

All power tends to corrupt; absolute power corrupts absolutely. Lord Acton

Instant Cocoa Mix

1 (8 quart) box dry milk powder
1 (12 ounce) jar non-dairy creamer
1 (16 ounce) can instant chocolate-flavored drink mix, divided
1¼ cups powdered sugar

- Combine all ingredients and store in airtight container.

- To serve, use ¼ cup cocoa mix per 1 cup of hot water.
  Yields 2 gallons.

Peppermint Hot Chocolate

3 cups hot milk, divided
8 small chocolate peppermint patties
1 cup half-and-half cream

- Combine ½ cup hot milk with chocolate peppermint patties and
  stir well.

- Add pinch of salt and remaining hot milk.

- Heat to simmering, but do not boil. Add half-and-half cream.
  Yields 1 quart.

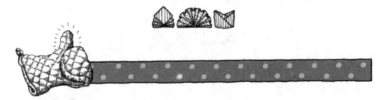

*Mount Whitney is 14,495 feet above
sea level and Bad Water in Death Valley
is 282 feet below sea level. These are
the highest and lowest points in the
contiguous U.S.*

Ladies' Spiced Coffee

1 cup instant coffee granules
4 teaspoons grated lemon peel
4 teaspoons ground cinnamon
1 teaspoon ground cloves

- Combine all ingredients in small jar and cover tightly.

- For each serving, spoon 2 teaspoons coffee mix into coffee cup and stir in ¾ cup boiling water. Yields 28 cups coffee.

TIP: Sweeten to taste.

Mocha Magic

4 cups brewed coffee
¼ cup sugar
4 cups milk
4 cups chocolate ice cream, softened

- Combine coffee and sugar in container and stir until sugar dissolves. Refrigerate for 2 hours.

- Just before serving, pour into small punch bowl. Add milk and mix well.

- Top with scoops of ice cream and stir well. Yields 3 quarts.

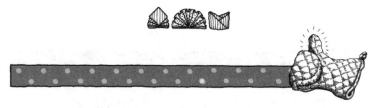

You don't choose your family. They are God's gift to you, as you are to them.
Desmond Tutu

Spanish Coffee

1 tablespoon sugar
4 cups hot, brewed coffee
¾ cup Kahlua® liqueur
Sweetened whipped cream or whipped topping

- Stir sugar into hot coffee and add Kahlua®.

- Pour into 4 serving cups. Top with whipped cream.
  Yields 1 quart.

Creamy Chocolate-Mint Fizz

¼ cup creme de menthe liqueur
¼ cup creme de cacao liqueur
1 (1 pint) carton vanilla ice cream
1 (1 pint) carton chocolate ice cream

- Place liqueurs into blender container.

- Add ice creams gradually and blend until smooth after
  each addition.

- Pour into glasses and serve immediately. Yields 1 quart.

Happy is the house that shelters a friend. Ralph Waldo Emerson

Frosted Chocolate Milk

2 pints coffee ice cream
½ cup chocolate syrup
¼ cup instant coffee granules
2 quarts milk, divided

- Beat ice cream, chocolate syrup, coffee and about half milk in blender. Beat until they blend well.

- Combine remaining milk and refrigerate before serving.

- Serve in frosted glasses. Yields 3 quarts.

Four-Fruit Slush

1 cup orange juice
1 ripe banana, peeled, thickly sliced
1 ripe peach, sliced
1 cup strawberries

- Pour orange juice into blender and add banana, peach, strawberries and 1 cup ice cubes.

- Blend on high speed until creamy. Yields 1½ pints.

Keep spot remover handy. Spills are inevitable. Don't let a few drops (or a glassful) of red wine ruin a good time.

Strawberry Smoothie

2 bananas, peeled, sliced
1 pint fresh strawberries, washed, quartered
1 (8 ounce) container strawberry yogurt
¼ cup orange juice

- Place all ingredients in blender. Process until smooth.
  Yields 1 quart.

Orange Sunrise Slushie

2 cups orange juice
½ cup instant, non-fat dry milk
¼ teaspoon almond extract
8 ice cubes

- Combine all ingredients in blender and process on high
  until mixture blends and thickens. Serve immediately.
  Yields 1½ pints.

Sunny Limeade Cooler

1½ pints lime sherbet, divided
1 (6 ounce) can frozen limeade concentrate
3 cups milk
Lime slices

- Beat lime sherbet in bowl and add concentrated limeade
  and milk.

- Blend all ingredients. Pour into glasses and top each with
  an additional scoop lime sherbet.

- Serve immediately. Garnish with lime slices. Yields 1½ quarts.

Pineapple-Strawberry Cooler

2 cups milk
1 (20 ounce) can crushed pineapple, chilled
½ pint vanilla ice cream
1 (1 pint) carton strawberry ice cream

- Combine milk, pineapple and vanilla ice cream in bowl.

- Mix just until they blend well. Pour into tall glasses and top with scoop of strawberry ice cream. Yields 1½ quarts.

Lemon-Banana Shake

1 (6 ounce) can frozen lemonade concentrate, thawed
1 cup chopped bananas
1 quart vanilla ice cream, divided
3 cups milk, divided

- Combine lemonade concentrate and bananas in bowl. Beat until mixture is thick.

- For each milkshake, add 1 scoop vanilla ice cream and ¼ cup lemon-banana mixture in bottom of glass.

- Fill glass two-thirds full milk and stir until it mixes well.

- Top off with 1 more scoop of ice cream. Yields 1 quart.

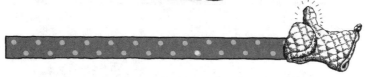

When you look at your life, the greatest happinesses are family happinesses. Joyce Brothers

Banana Split Float

2 ripe bananas, mashed
3 cups milk
1 (10 ounce) package frozen sweetened strawberries, thawed
1½ pints chocolate ice cream, divided

- Place bananas in blender and add milk, strawberries and ½ pint chocolate ice cream. Beat just until they blend well.

- Pour into tall, chilled glasses and top each with scoop of chocolate ice cream. Yields 1 quart.

Chocolate-Yogurt Malt

4 cups frozen vanilla yogurt
1 cup chocolate milk
¼ cup instant chocolate malted-milk drink
Mini chocolate chips

- Process yogurt, milk and malted-milk drink in blender until smooth and stop to scrape sides.

- Serve immediately.

- Top with mini-chocolate chips. Yields 5 cups.

When Georgia became the thirteenth colony, every man, woman and child was promised 64 quarts of molasses if they stayed one year. Molasses was the sweetener of choice until after World War I when sugar became less expensive.

Peanut Power Smoothie

2 bananas, cut up
½ cup frozen orange juice concentrate, thawed
¼ cup peanut butter
¼ cup milk

- Combine all ingredients in blender. Cover and blend until smooth.

- Add 1 cup ice cubes and blend until smooth. Yields 1 pint.

Toffee Milk Shake

1 (1 pint) carton vanilla ice cream, divided
1 cup milk
½ cup chocolate-coated toffee bits

- Combine half ice cream and milk in blender. Cover and blend until smooth.

- Add in remaining ice cream. Cover and blend until desired consistency.

- Add toffee bits and process briefly with on/off pulse to mix. Yields 1½ pints.

Natural peanut butter is made without sugar or hydrogenated oils and has a thicker texture than regular peanut butter.

Kahlua Frosty

1 cup Kahlua® liqueur
1 (1 pint) carton vanilla ice cream
1 cup half-and-half cream
¼ teaspoon almond extract

- Combine all ingredients and 1 heaping cup ice cubes in blender.

- Blend until smooth. Serve immediately. Yields 1 quart.

Amaretto

3 cups sugar
1 pint vodka
3 tablespoons almond extract
1 tablespoon vanilla

- Combine sugar and 2¼ cups water in large pan. Bring mixture to a boil.

- Reduce heat. Simmer for 5 minutes and stir occasionally. Remove from stove.

- Add vodka, almond extract and vanilla. Stir to mix. Store in airtight jar. Yields 2 pints.

You have enemies? Good. That means you've stood up for something, sometime in your life. Winston Churchill

Breads

Kneady Biscuits

2 cups flour
1 tablespoon baking powder
½ teaspoon salt
1 (8 ounce) carton whipping cream

- Preheat oven to 375°.

- Combine flour, baking powder and salt in bowl.

- In separate bowl, beat whipping cream only until it holds its shape.

- Combine flour mixture and cream and mix with fork. Put dough on lightly floured board and knead it for about 1 minute.

- Pat dough to ¾-inch thickness. Cut out biscuits with small biscuit cutter or small glass.

- Place on sprayed baking sheet and bake for about 12 minutes or until light brown. Yields 10 biscuits.

Crazy Beer Biscuits

3¼ cups biscuit mix
1 teaspoon sugar
1⅔ cups beer

- Preheat oven to 400°.

- Combine all ingredients and ¼ teaspoon salt in bowl and spoon into 12 sprayed muffin cups.

- Bake for 15 to 20 minutes until golden. Yields 20 biscuits.

Quick Sour Cream Biscuits

⅓ cup club soda
⅓ cup sour cream
½ tablespoon sugar
2 cups biscuit mix

- Preheat oven to 400°.

- Combine all ingredients in bowl with fork just until dry ingredients are moist.

- Turn bowl onto lightly floured board and knead gently several times.

- Roll dough into 1-inch thickness and cut with biscuit cutter or small glass.

- Place dough in sprayed 9 x 13-inch baking pan.

- Bake for 12 to 14 minutes or until golden brown. Yields 10 to 12 biscuits.

Garlic Biscuits

5 cups biscuit mix
1 cup shredded cheddar cheese
1 (14 ounce) can chicken broth with roasted garlic
Butter

- Preheat oven to 425°.

- Mix all ingredients in bowl to form soft dough. Drop heaping teaspoonfuls of dough onto sprayed baking sheet.

- Bake for 10 minutes or until slightly brown. Serve hot and with butter. Yields 30 biscuits.

Maple Syrup Biscuits

2¼ cups baking mix
⅔ cup milk
1½ cups maple syrup
Butter

- Preheat oven to 425°.

- Combine baking mix and milk. Stir just until moist.

- On floured surface, roll dough into ½-inch thickness. Cut with 2-inch biscuit cutter or small glass.

- Pour syrup into 7 x 11-inch baking dish. Place biscuits on top of syrup.

- Bake for 13 to 15 minutes or until biscuits are golden brown. Serve warm and with butter. Yields 10 to 12 biscuits.

Speedy Biscuits

6 tablespoons shortening
3 cups flour
1 cup milk
Butter

- Preheat oven to 400°.

- Cut shortening into flour with pastry cutter or fork. Add milk and mix until dough forms a ball. Knead until dough is smooth.

- Place on floured surface and flatten slightly. Cut with floured biscuit cutter, place in sprayed pan and turn over to grease both sides of biscuits.

- Bake for 10 to 12 minutes. Yields 15 to 20 biscuits.

Easy Date Biscuits

1 cup chopped dates
2 cups biscuit mix
½ cup shredded American cheese
¾ cup milk

- Preheat oven to 400°.

- Combine dates, biscuit mix and cheese in bowl.

- Add milk and stir well to get moderately soft dough. Drop teaspoonfuls of dough onto sprayed baking sheet.

- Bake for 12 to 15 minutes. Serve hot. Yields 8 to 12 biscuits.

Hot Cheese Biscuits

1 (5 ounce) jar Old English cheese spread
¼ cup (½ stick) butter, softened
1 cup flour

- Combine cheese spread and butter in bowl and mix well. Add flour and a little salt. Mix well.

- Roll into small balls and refrigerate for 1 hour.

- When ready to bake, preheat oven to 400°.

- Place balls onto baking sheet.

- Bake for 10 minutes. Balls will flatten as they cook. Serve hot. Yields 4 to 6 biscuits.

Sausage-Cheese Biscuits

1 (8 ounce) package shredded cheddar cheese
1 pound hot bulk pork sausage
2 cups biscuit mix
¾ cup milk

- Preheat oven to 400°.

- Combine cheese, sausage and biscuit mix in bowl.

- Drop tablespoonfuls of dough onto baking sheet.

- Bake until light brown. Serve hot. Yields 10 to 12 biscuits.

Strawberry Topping for Biscuits

This is delicious over hot biscuits.

3½ cups sugar
1 (10 ounce) package frozen strawberries, thawed
1 (6 ounce) can frozen orange juice concentrate, thawed
2 tablespoons lemon juice

- Combine sugar and strawberries in large saucepan and mix
  well. Over high heat bring to a full rolling boil for 1 minute
  and stir constantly.

- Remove from heat and stir in orange juice concentrate and
  lemon juice. Return to heat, bring to a boil for 1 minute and
  stir constantly.

- Skim foam off top. Add red food coloring, if you like.

- Pour into jelly glasses and seal with hot paraffin. Yields 2 cups.

Mademoiselle Biscuits

2 cups biscuit mix
¼ cup milk
1 (8 ounce) container French onion dip
2 tablespoons finely minced green onion

- Preheat oven to 400°.

- Combine all ingredients in bowl until soft dough forms. Drop tablespoonfuls of dough onto sprayed baking sheet.

- Bake for 10 minutes or until light golden brown. Yields 8 to 12 biscuits.

Old South Sweet Potato Biscuits

1 (15 ounce) can sweet potatoes, drained
1 tablespoon sugar
¼ cup milk
1½ cups biscuit mix

- Preheat oven to 450°.

- Mash sweet potatoes in bowl, add sugar and milk and beat until creamy. Pour in biscuit mix and stir with fork until most lumps dissolve.

- Pour mixture onto floured, wax paper and knead 5 to 6 times. Press down to about ½-inch thick and cut out biscuits with biscuit cutter or small glass.

- Bake for 10 to 12 minutes onto baking sheet. Yields 8 to 12 biscuits.

Toasted French Bread

1 loaf French bread
½ cup (1 stick) butter, softened
¾ cup shredded parmesan cheese
1½ teaspoons hot sauce

- Preheat oven to 325°.

- Slice bread in half lengthwise and quarter.

- Combine butter, parmesan cheese and hot sauce in bowl. Spread entire mixture on top of slices. Place on baking sheet.

- Cook for 25 minutes or until thoroughly hot and light brown on top. Yields 8 slices.

Parmesan Bread Deluxe

1 loaf Italian bread
½ cup refrigerated creamy Caesar dressing and dip
⅓ cup grated parmesan cheese
3 tablespoons finely chopped green onions

- Cut 24 (½ inch) thick slices from bread. Reserve remaining bread for other use.

- Combine dressing, cheese and onion in small bowl. Spread 1 teaspoon dressing mixture on each bread slice.

- Place bread on baking sheet. Broil 4 inches from heat until golden brown. Serve warm. Yields 24 slices.

Buttery Ranch Bread

1 loaf French bread
½ cup (1 stick) butter, softened
1 tablespoon ranch-style dressing mix
1 tablespoon mayonnaise, optional

- Preheat oven to 350º.

- Cut loaf in half horizontally. Blend butter, dressing mix and mayonnaise in bowl. Spread butter mixture on bread.

- Wrap bread in foil. Bake for 15 minutes. Yields 10 to 16 slices.

Easy Cheese Bread

1 (8 ounce) package shredded, sharp cheddar cheese
1 cup mayonnaise
1 (1 ounce) packet ranch dressing mix
10 (1 inch) slices French bread

- Combine cheese, mayonnaise and dressing mix in bowl.

- Spread on bread slices and heat in oven until brown, about 10 to 15 minutes. Yields 10 slices.

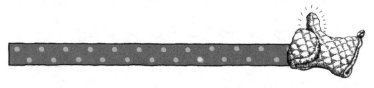

My mother was the making of me. She was so true, so sure of me and I felt that I had someone to live for, someone I must not disappoint. Thomas Edison

Green Chili-Cheese Bread

1 loaf Italian bread
½ cup (1 stick) butter, melted
1 (4 ounce) can diced green chilies, drained
¾ cup grated Monterey Jack cheese

- Preheat oven to 350°.

- Slice bread horizontally almost all the way through.

- Combine melted butter, green chilies and cheese in bowl. Spread between bread slices.

- Cover loaf with foil. Bake for 25 minutes. Slice and serve hot. Yields 10 to 16 slices.

Fancy Sausage Cornbread

1 (10 ounce) can cream of celery soup
2 eggs
1 (8 ounce) package corn muffin mix
⅓ pound pork sausage, crumbled, cooked

- Preheat oven to 375°.

- Combine soup, eggs and ¼ cup water or milk in medium bowl.

- Stir in corn muffin mix just until it blends. Fold in sausage.

- Pour mixture into sprayed 9-inch square baking pan.

- Bake for 25 minutes or until golden brown. Cut into squares. Yields 9 to 16 squares.

Mexican Cornbread

1 (8 ounce) box Mexican cubed Velveeta® cheese, cubed
¾ cup milk
2 (8 ounce) packages corn muffin mix
2 eggs, beaten

- Preheat oven to 375°.

- Melt cheese with milk in saucepan over low heat and stir
  constantly. Combine corn muffin mix and eggs in bowl. Fold
  in cheese and mix just until moist.

- Pour into sprayed, floured 9 x 13-inch baking pan.

- Bake for about 25 minutes or until light brown. Yields 12 to
  16 squares.

Quickie Ginger Muffins

1 (16 ounce) box gingerbread mix
1 egg
2 (1.5 ounce) boxes seedless raisins
Butter

- Preheat oven to 350°.

- Combine gingerbread mix, 1¼ cups lukewarm water and egg in
  bowl and mix well. Stir in raisins.

- Pour into sprayed muffin cups to half full.

- Bake for 20 minutes or when toothpick inserted in center comes
  out clean. Serve warm and with butter. Yields 8 to 12 muffins.

Blueberry-Orange Muffins

1 (16 ounce) package blueberry muffin mix with blueberries
2 egg whites
½ cup orange juice
Orange marmalade

- Preheat oven to 375°.

- Wash blueberries with cold water and drain.

- Combine muffin mix, egg whites and orange juice in bowl and break up any lumps.

- Gently fold blueberries into batter. Pour into muffin cups (with paper liners) about half full.

- Bake for 18 to 20 minutes or until toothpick inserted in center comes out clean.

- Spoon orange marmalade over top of hot muffins. Yields 6 to 10 muffins.

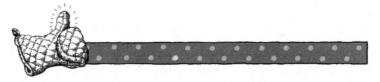

I am only one, but I am one. I cannot do everything, but I can do something. And because I cannot do everything, I will not refuse to do the something that I can do. What I can do, I should do. And what I should do, by the grace of God, I will do. Edward Everett Hale

Breakfast
&
Brunch

Pepe's Sunrise Tacos

4 eggs, scrambled, divided
½ cup shredded cheddar cheese, divided
½ cup salsa, divided
2 flour tortillas, divided

- Scramble eggs in sprayed skillet.

- For each taco, spread half scrambled eggs, ¼ cup cheese and
  ¼ cup salsa on tortilla and roll. Yields 2 tacos.

Lickety-Split Breakfast Tacos

4 eggs, beaten
4 flour tortillas
1 cup cooked, chopped ham
1 cup shredded cheddar cheese

- Scramble eggs in skillet. Lay tortillas flat and spoon eggs evenly
  on tortillas.

- Sprinkle with ham and cheese and roll to enclose filling.

- Place tacos in microwave-safe dish. Microwave for about
  30 seconds or until cheese melts. Serve immediately. Yields 4.

*Take away the heritage of a people and
they are easily persuaded.* Karl Marx

Bacon-Cheese Stromboli

1 (10 ounce) tube refrigerated pizza dough
¾ cup shredded cheddar cheese
¾ cup shredded mozzarella cheese
6 bacon strips, cooked, crumbled

- Preheat oven to 400°.

- Roll dough into 12-inch circle on unsprayed baking sheet.

- On one-half of dough, sprinkle cheeses and bacon to within ½-inch of edge.

- Fold dough over filling and pinch edges to seal.

- Bake for about 10 minutes or until golden. Cut in wedges. Serves 4.

Chile Rellenos

2 (7 ounce) cans diced green chilies, drained
1 (16 ounce) package shredded Monterey Jack cheese
4 eggs, beaten
½ cup milk

- Preheat oven to 350°.

- Layer half green chilies, half cheese, then remaining chilies and cheese in 7 x 11-inch baking dish.

- Combine eggs and milk in small bowl and mix well.

- Pour over layers of cheese and green chilies.

- Bake for 30 minutes or until light brown and set. Cool for 5 minutes before cutting into squares. Serves 4.

Corned Beef Hash Bake

2 (15 ounce) cans corned beef hash, slightly warmed
Butter
6 - 8 eggs
⅓ cup half-and-half cream

- Preheat oven to 350º.

- Spread corned beef hash in sprayed 9 x 13-inch pan. Pat down with back of spoon and make 6 to 8 deep hollows in hash large enough for egg to fit.

- Fill hollows with tiny dab of butter.

- Pour 1 egg into each hollow and cover with about 1 tablespoon or so of half-and-half cream.

- Bake for 15 to 20 minutes or until eggs set as desired. Divide into squares to serve. Yields 8 squares.

A Better Scramble

1 (10 ounce) can cheddar cheese soup
8 eggs, lightly beaten
2 tablespoons butter
Snipped chives

- Pour soup into bowl and stir until smooth. Add eggs and a little pepper and mix well.

- Melt butter in skillet. Pour in egg mixture and scramble over low heat until set.

- Sprinkle with chives. Serves 3 to 4.

Breakfast Wake-Up

2 (7 ounce) cans diced green chilies
12 eggs
2 (16 ounce) packages shredded cheddar cheese, divided
Salsa

- Preheat oven to 350°.

- Drain green chilies and save liquid. In separate bowl, beat eggs with liquid from green chilies.

- Spread half cheese on bottom of sprayed 9 x 13-inch baking pan and layer chilies over this. Top with remaining cheese.

- Pour eggs over top and bake for 45 minutes. Serve with salsa. Serves 4 to 6.

Cheesy Scrambled Eggs

2 tablespoons butter
8 eggs
1 (4 ounce) can diced green chilies
½ cup shredded cheddar cheese

- Melt butter in skillet.

- Beat remaining ingredients well in bowl and pour into skillet.

- Cook and stir until set. Serves 6.

What was Snow White's brother's name? Egg White! Get the yoke?

Simple Baked Eggs

4 eggs
4 tablespoons cream, divided
4 tablespoons cracker crumbs, divided
4 tablespoons shredded cheddar cheese, divided

- Preheat oven to 325°.

- Spray 4 muffin cups. Crack eggs open and place 1 in each of 4 muffin cups.

- Add 1 tablespoon each of cream, crumbs and cheese for each egg.

- Bake for 12 to 20 minutes until eggs are set. Yields 4.

TIP: As many eggs as required may be prepared at the same time.

Easy Pecan Waffles

2 cups self-rising flour
½ cup canola oil
½ cup milk
⅔ cup finely chopped pecans

- Preheat waffle iron. Combine flour, oil and milk in bowl. Beat until they mix well. Stir in chopped pecans.

- Pour approximately ¾ cup batter into hot waffle iron and bake until brown and crispy. Serves 3 to 4.

Light, Crispy Waffles

2 cups biscuit mix
1 egg
½ cup canola oil
1⅓ cups club soda

- Preheat waffle iron. Combine all ingredients in bowl and stir with whisk.

- Pour just enough batter to cover waffle iron. Serves 3 to 4.

TIP: To have waffles for a "company weekend", make up all waffles in advance. Freeze separately on baking sheet and place in large plastic bags. To heat, warm at 350° for about 10 minutes.

French Toast Flash

4 eggs
1 cup whipping cream
2 thick slices bread, cut into 3 strips
Powdered sugar, sifted

- Preheat oven to 325°.

- Place a little oil in skillet. Beat eggs, cream and pinch of salt.

- Dip bread into batter and allow batter to soak in.

- Fry bread in skillet until brown, turn and fry on other side.

- Transfer to baking sheet. Bake for about 4 minutes or until they puff. Sprinkle with powdered sugar. Serves 3.

TIP: Use a little canola oil to fry bread in skillet.

Blueberry Coffee Cake

1 (16 ounce) package blueberry muffin mix with blueberries
⅓ cup sour cream
1 egg
⅔ cup powdered sugar

- Preheat oven to 400°.

- Stir muffin mix, sour cream, egg and ½ cup water in bowl.

- Rinse blueberries and gently fold into batter. Pour into sprayed 7 x 11-inch baking dish.

- Bake for about 25 minutes.

- Mix powdered sugar and 1 tablespoon water in small bowl and drizzle over coffee cake. Serves 6 to 8.

Palace Pineapple Coffee Cake

1 (18 ounce) box butter cake mix
½ cup canola oil
4 eggs, slightly beaten
1 (20 ounce) can pineapple pie filling

- Preheat oven to 350°.

- Combine cake mix, oil and eggs in bowl. Beat until they mix well. Pour batter into sprayed, floured 9 x 13-inch baking pan.

- Bake for 45 to 50 minutes or until toothpick inserted in center comes out clean.

- Punch holes in cake with knife about 2 inches apart. Spread pineapple pie filling over cake while it is still hot. Serves 6 to 8.

Sticky Pecan Rolls

1 (12 count) package brown-and-serve dinner rolls
4 tablespoons butter
⅔ cup packed brown sugar
24 pecan halves

- Preheat oven to 350°.

- Place 1 roll in each of 12 well sprayed muffin cups.

- Cut an "x" in top of each roll.

- Combine brown sugar and butter in saucepan, melt and mix well. Spoon mixture over rolls.

- Tuck 2 pecan halves in "x" on each roll. Bake for 20 minutes or until light brown. Serves 4 to 6.

Spiced Pears

1 (15 ounce) can pear halves
⅓ cup packed brown sugar
¾ teaspoon ground nutmeg
¾ teaspoon ground cinnamon

- Drain pears, reserve syrup and set pears aside.

- Place syrup, brown sugar, nutmeg and cinnamon in saucepan and bring to a boil. Reduce heat, simmer for 5 to 8 minutes and stir frequently.

- Add pears and simmer for 5 minutes longer or until thoroughly hot. Serves 2 to 4.

Melon Boats

2 cantaloupes, chilled
4 cups red and green seedless grapes, chilled
1 cup mayonnaise
⅓ cup frozen concentrated orange juice

- Cut each melon into 6 lengthwise sections and remove seeds and peel. Place on separate salad plates.

- Heap grapes over and around cantaloupe slices.

- Combine mayonnaise and juice concentrate in bowl and mix well. Ladle over fruit. Yields 12 boats.

Strawberry Fields Butter

Strawberry butter is delicious on biscuits, muffins or breads.

1 (10 ounce) package frozen strawberries with juice
1 cup (2 sticks) butter, softened
1 cup powdered sugar
Breakfast breads or toast

- Place strawberries, butter and powdered sugar in food processor or mixer and process until mixed.

- Serve on breakfast breads or toast. Yields 1 pint.

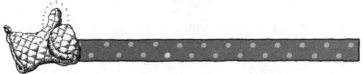

A few germs never hurt anyone.
Anonymous

Sweet Orange Butter

Great on biscuits and hot rolls.

⅔ cup butter, softened
¼ cup frozen orange juice concentrate, thawed
1 (1 pound) box powdered sugar
1 teaspoon dried orange zest

- Blend all ingredients with mixer or processor. Store in refrigerator. Yields 1½ pints.

Yummy Praline Spread

½ cup (1 stick) butter, softened
1 cup packed brown sugar
½ cup finely chopped pecans
8 – 10 Bread slices

- Combine butter, sugar and pecans in bowl. Spread on bread slices.

- Toast in broiler until brown and bubbly. Yields 8 to 10.

I never did give them hell. I just told the truth and they thought it was hell.
Harry S. Truman

Fruity Ambrosia Spread

This is a great dip for fruits, too.

1 (11 ounce) can mandarin orange sections, drained
1 (8 ounce) carton soft cream cheese with pineapple, softened
¼ cup flaked coconut, toasted
¼ cup slivered almonds, chopped, toasted

- Chop orange sections and set aside.

- Beat cream cheese, coconut and almonds in bowl and blend well. Gently fold in orange sections. Refrigerate. Yields 1 pint.

TIP: Spread on date-nut bread, banana bread, etc.

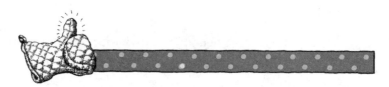

Spanish colonists introduced to North America almonds, apples, apricots, bananas, barley, beans, cherries, chickpeas, chilies, citrons, dates, figs, grapes, lemons, lentils, limes, maize, olives, nectarines, oranges, peaches, pears, plums, pomegranates, quinces, tomatias, walnuts, wheat, chickens, cows, donkeys, goats, horses, sheep and domesticated turkey. Spanish colonists also introduced saffron, olive oil and anise.

Soups, Salads
&
Sandwiches

Speedy Taco Soup

1 (12 ounce) can chicken with liquid
1 (14 ounce) can chicken broth
1 (16 ounce) jar mild thick-and-chunky salsa
1 (15 ounce) can ranch-style (chili) beans

- Combine chicken, broth, salsa and beans in large saucepan.

- Bring to a boil, reduce heat and simmer for 15 minutes. Serves 4.

TIP: *If you want a heartier soup, add 1 (15 ounce) can whole
kernel corn.*

Cream of Turkey Soup

1 (10 ounce) can cream of celery soup
1 (10 ounce) can cream of chicken soup
2 soup cans milk
1 cup cooked, finely diced turkey

- Combine all ingredients in large saucepan and serve hot. Serves 4.

*Did you know that lettuce loves fat?
Fat can be removed from hot soup
by floating a large lettuce leaf on the
surface.*

Anchors Aweigh Soup

3 (15 ounce) cans navy beans with liquid
1 cup cooked, chopped ham
1 large onion, chopped
½ teaspoon garlic powder

- Combine beans, ham, onion and garlic powder in large saucepan.

- Add 1 cup water and bring to boil. Simmer until onion is tender-crisp. Serves 4 to 6.

TIP: *This is great with hot buttered cornbread. The small box of Jiffy®*
    cornbread mix is very good, fast and plenty easy.

Spicy Tomato Soup

2 (10 ounce) cans tomato soup
1 (15 ounce) can Mexican stewed tomatoes
Sour cream
½ pound bacon, fried, drained, crumbled

- Combine soup and stewed tomatoes in saucepan and heat.

- To serve, place dollop of sour cream on each bowl of soup and sprinkle crumbled bacon over sour cream. Serves 4.

Need to thicken your soup? Adding a
little pasta or mashed potato flakes is a
great way to add bulk to your soup.

Farmhouse Bacon-Potato Soup

2 (14 ounce) cans chicken broth seasoned with garlic
2 potatoes, peeled, cubed
1 onion, finely chopped
6 strips bacon, cooked, crumbled

- Combine broth, potatoes and onion in large saucepan. Bring to a boil, reduce heat to medium and cook for about 10 minutes or until potatoes are tender.

- Ladle into bowls and sprinkle with crumbled bacon. Serves 4.

Super Supper Gumbo

1 (10 ounce) can pepper pot soup
1 (10 ounce) can chicken gumbo soup
1 (6 ounce) can white crabmeat, flaked
1 (6 ounce) can tiny shrimp, drained

- Combine all ingredients with 1½ soup cans water in saucepan.

- Cover and simmer for 15 minutes. Serves 4.

Chicken, U.S.A.
Four cities in the United States have the word "chicken" in their names: Chicken, Alaska; Chicken Bristle, Illinois; Chicken Bristle, Kentucky; and Chicken Town, Pennsylvania.

Spiked Crab Soup

1 (1 ounce) packet onion soup mix
1 (6 ounce) can crabmeat with liquid, flaked
1 (8 ounce) carton whipping cream
½ cup white wine

- Dissolve soup mix with 2 cups water in saucepan.

- Add crabmeat, crab liquid and whipping cream.

- Heat, but do not boil, reduce heat and simmer for 20 minutes.

- Stir in wine, heat and serve warm. Serves 4.

TIP: *Season to taste with a little salt and pepper.*

Napoleon Tomato Soup

1 (10 ounce) can tomato bisque soup
2 (10 ounce) cans French onion soup
Croutons
Grated parmesan cheese

- Combine soups and 2 soup cans water in saucepan. Heat thoroughly.

- Serve in bowls topped with croutons and a sprinkle of cheese. Serves 4.

Salty soup? If your sauce, soup or stew is too salty, add a peeled potato to the pot, and it will absorb the extra salt.

Sunny Summer Squash Soup

2 pounds fresh, yellow squash, thinly sliced
1 onion, chopped
1 (14 ounce) can chicken broth
1 (8 ounce) carton sour cream

- Simmer squash and onions in broth in saucepan until very tender. Refrigerate.

- Just before serving, add sour cream. Serve cold. Serves 4.

TIP: *Season to taste with salt and pepper.*

Chicken Caesar Salad

4 boneless, skinless chicken breast halves, grilled
1 (10 ounce) package romaine salad greens
½ cup shredded parmesan cheese
¾ cup Caesar or Italian dressing

- Cut chicken breasts into strips. Combine chicken, salad greens and cheese in large bowl.

- When ready to serve, toss with dressing. Serves 6.

*Did you know ice cubes love fat?
Eliminate fat from soup by dropping ice
cubes into your soup pot. As you stir,
the fat will cling to the cubes.*

Mexican Chicken Salad

3 - 4 boneless skinless chicken breast, cooked, cubed
1 (15 ounce) can chick-peas (garbanzo beans), drained
1 red bell pepper, seeded, diced
1 cup chopped celery

- Combine all ingredients in bowl and serve with Sour Cream-Cilantro Dressing.

Sour Cream-Cilantro Dressing

1½ cups sour cream
2 tablespoons chili sauce
2 teaspoons ground cumin
1 small bunch fresh cilantro, minced

- Combine all ingredients in bowl.

- Pour over chicken salad and toss. Refrigerate before serving. Serves 6.

Chicken/Egg Debate Finally Resolved

According to National Geographic, scientists have settled the old dispute over which came first - the chicken or the egg. They say that reptiles were laying eggs thousands of years before chickens appeared, and the first chicken came from an egg laid by a bird that was not quite a chicken. Clearly, the egg came first.

Apple-Walnut Chicken Salad

3 - 4 boneless skinless chicken breast halves, cooked, cubed
2 tart green apples, peeled, chopped
½ cup chopped pitted dates
1 cup minced celery

- Mix all ingredients in bowl. Toss with Walnut-Mayo Dressing.

Walnut-Mayo Dressing

½ cup chopped walnuts
⅓ cup sour cream
⅓ cup mayonnaise
1 tablespoon lemon juice

- Preheat oven to 300°.

- Toast walnuts for 10 minutes. Mix sour cream, mayonnaise and
  lemon juice in bowl. Mix with walnuts. Pour over chicken salad
  and toss. Refrigerate. Serves 6.

You don't have to have lettuce or greens to make a salad. For a quick, "right-out-of-the-refrigerator" salad, mix broccoli, cauliflower, celery, cucumbers, tomatoes, green beans and anything else you find on the shelves that might work. Add your favorite dressing and toss.

Black Bean-Chicken Salad

2 - 3 boneless skinless chicken breasts, cooked, cubed
1 (15 ounce) can black beans, drained
1 bunch green onions, chopped
1 cup chopped celery

- Blend all ingredients in bowl and toss with Cumin Vinaigrette Dressing.

Cumin Vinaigrette Dressing

¾ cup extra light olive oil
¼ cup lemon juice
2 teaspoons dijon-style mustard
1 teaspoon ground cumin

- Combine all ingredients in bowl.

- Toss with Black Bean-Chicken Salad and refrigerate. Serves 6.

Derby Chicken Salad

3 - 4 boneless skinless chicken breast halves, cooked, cubed
2 avocados, peeled, diced
2 tomatoes, diced, drained
Italian salad dressing

- Combine all ingredients in bowl.

- When ready to serve, pour dressing over salad and toss. Refrigerate. Serves 6.

Open Sesame Salad

1 large head romaine lettuce
2 tablespoons sesame seeds, toasted
6 strips bacon, fried, crumbled
Creamy Italian salad dressing

- Wash and dry lettuce. Tear into bite-size pieces in bowl.

- When ready to serve, sprinkle sesame seeds and bacon over lettuce and toss with dressing. Serves 3 to 4.

Festive Red and Green Salad

2 (10 ounce) packages fresh spinach, stemmed
1 quart fresh strawberries, halved
½ cup slivered almonds, toasted
1 (8 ounce) bottle poppy seed salad dressing

- Tear spinach into small pieces and add strawberries and almonds.

- Refrigerate until ready to serve. Toss with poppy seed dressing. Serves 6.

TIP: *Toasting almonds brings out their flavor. Spread almond slivers on baking sheet and bake in oven at 200° for about 1 hour; stir once or twice. It's worth the effort.*

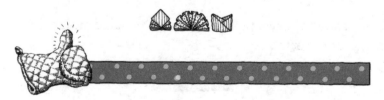

Anger is one letter short of danger.
Eleanor Roosevelt

Strawberry-Spinach Salad

1 (10 ounce) package fresh spinach, washed, stemmed
1 small jicama, peeled, julienned
1 pint fresh strawberries, stemmed, halved
2½ cups fresh bean sprouts

• Combine spinach, jicama, strawberries and bean sprouts in large
  bowl. Toss and serve immediately. Serves 4.

TIP: *If you want to add a dressing, try poppy seed or any vinaigrette.*

Oriental Spinach Salad

1 (10 ounce) package fresh spinach
1 (16 ounce) can bean sprouts, drained
8 slices bacon, cooked crisp, drained
1 (11 ounce) can water chestnuts, chopped

• Combine spinach and bean sprouts in bowl.

• When ready to serve, add crumbled bacon and water chestnuts.
  Serves 4.

TIP: *Any vinaigrette or mist is delicious with this salad. The*
      homemade vinaigrette recipe following this salad is excellent.

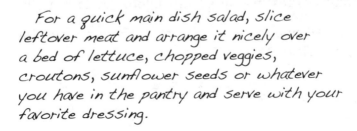

*For a quick main dish salad, slice
leftover meat and arrange it nicely over
a bed of lettuce, chopped veggies,
croutons, sunflower seeds or whatever
you have in the pantry and serve with your
favorite dressing.*

Homemade Vinaigrette Dressing

⅔ cup salad olive oil
⅓ cup red wine vinegar
1 tablespoon seasoned salt

- Mix all ingredients and refrigerate. Yields 1 cup.

Select Spinach Salad

1 (10 ounce) package fresh spinach
2 eggs, hard-boiled, sliced
1 (14 ounce) can bean sprouts, drained
1 (11 ounce) can sliced water chestnuts, chopped

- Combine all salad ingredients in large bowl. Serves 4.

TIP: *The Sweet Oil and Vinegar Dressing recipe following this salad is delicious.*

Sweet Oil and Vinegar Dressing

¾ cup olive oil
⅓ cup sugar
¼ cup ketchup
3 tablespoons red wine vinegar

- Combine all dressing ingredients in bowl and mix well.

- Use desired amount of dressing and refrigerate remaining dressing. Yields 1 cup.

Living Sprouts Mix

1 (10 ounce) package fresh baby spinach
1 (15 ounce) can bean sprouts, drained
8 slices bacon, cooked crisp, crumbled
1 (11 ounce) can sliced water chestnuts, chopped

• Combine spinach and bean sprouts in bowl.

• When ready to serve, add crumbled bacon and water chestnuts. Serves 4.

TIP: Your favorite vinaigrette will work well if you want a dressing.

Broccoli-Pepperoni Crunch

1 (1 pound) bunch broccoli
½ pound fresh mushrooms, sliced
1 (3 ounce) package sliced pepperoni, chopped
Italian dressing

• Cut off broccoli florets. Combine broccoli, mushrooms, cheese and pepperoni in bowl. Toss with Italian dressing.

• Refrigerate for at least 8 hours before serving. Serves 4.

TIP: Adding ¾ cup diced Swiss cheese gives this salad more color and texture, but it is not mandatory. This is great just like it is.

To quickly slice mushrooms, small tomatoes, radishes and similar firm fruits and vegetables, use an egg slicer.

Marinated Brussels Sprouts

2 (10 ounce) boxes frozen brussels sprouts
1 cup Italian dressing
1 cup seeded, chopped green bell pepper
½ cup chopped onion

- Pierce box of brussels sprouts and cook in microwave for 7 minutes.

- Mix Italian dressing, bell pepper and onion in bowl.

- Pour over brussels sprouts and marinate for at least 24 hours. Drain to serve. Serves 6.

Red Cabbage Slaw

1 large head red cabbage
2 onions, finely chopped
½ cup coleslaw dressing
½ cup French salad dressing

- Slice cabbage and combine with onions in bowl.

- In separate bowl, combine dressings and toss with cabbage and onions. Refrigerate. Serves 4.

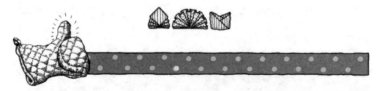

Nobody can do for little children what grandparents do. Grandparents sort of sprinkle stardust over the lives of little children. Alex Haley

Kwik Karrot Salad

3 cups finely grated carrots
1 (8 ounce) can crushed pineapple, drained
1 tablespoon sugar
⅓ cup mayonnaise

- Combine carrots, pineapple and sugar in bowl. Toss with mayonnaise and mix well.

- Refrigerate. Serves 4 to 6.

Marinated Onion Rings

2 pounds white onion, thinly sliced
1 cup sugar
2 cups white vinegar
½ teaspoon salt

- Cover onions with boiling water, let stand for 5 minutes. Drain.

- Combine sugar, vinegar and salt in bowl and pour over onions. Refrigerate. Serves 6.

Save some time by slicing or chopping vegetables all at one time, then storing them in plastic bags in the refrigerator. When you're ready to use them, just pull out the bag and use what you need. You'll be surprised how nice it is.

Onion-Bean Medley

1 (15 ounce) can whole green beans
1 (15 ounce) can yellow wax beans
½ cup finely chopped red onion
¼ cup slivered almonds

- Combine all ingredients in bowl and mix with dressing.

Dijon Vinaigrette:

¼ cup olive oil
1 tablespoon white vinegar
1 teaspoon sugar
2 teaspoons dijon-style mustard

- Combine all ingredients in bowl. Pour over bean and onion salad.

- Refrigerate for at least 1 hour before serving. Serves 4.

Crunchy Pea Salad

1 (16 ounce) package frozen green peas, thawed
1 head cauliflower, cut into bite-size pieces
1 (8 ounce) carton sour cream
1 (1 ounce) packet ranch salad dressing mix

- Combine peas and cauliflower in large bowl.

- In separate bowl, combine sour cream and salad dressing. Toss with vegetables. Refrigerate. Serves 6 to 8.

Sunshine Salad

2 (15 ounce) cans Mexicorn®, drained
2 (15 ounce) cans peas, drained
1 (15 ounce) can kidney beans, rinsed, drained
1 (8 ounce) bottle Italian dressing

- Combine corn, peas and beans in large bowl.

- Pour salad dressing over vegetables and refrigerate for several hours. Serves 4.

TIP: *If you don't have Mexicorn® in the pantry, use regular canned corn. If you don't have peas, use green beans. Sometimes we just have to "color outside the lines."*

Fusilli Pasta Quick-Fix

1 (16 ounce) package fusilli or corkscrew pasta
1 (16 ounce) package frozen broccoli-cauliflower combination
1 (8 ounce) package cubed mozzarella cheese
1 (8 ounce) bottle Catalina salad dressing

- Cook pasta according to package directions. Drain and cool.

- Cook vegetables in microwave according to package directions. Drain and cool.

- Combine pasta, vegetables and cheese cubes in large bowl.

- Toss with Catalina dressing. Refrigerate for several hours before serving. Serves 6 to 8.

Hometown Deviled Eggs

6 eggs, hard-boiled
2 tablespoons sweet pickle relish
3 tablespoons mayonnaise
½ teaspoon mustard

- Peel eggs and cut in half lengthwise. Take yolks and mash with fork in bowl.

- Add relish, mayonnaise and mustard to yolks. Place yolk mixture back into egg white halves. Yields 12.

TIP: *Some people like to sprinkle paprika over deviled eggs to give them color.*

Apple-Pineapple Salad

1 (6 ounce) package lemon gelatin
1 (15 ounce) can pineapple tidbits with liquid
1 cup diced apples with peels
1 cup chopped pecans

- Dissolve gelatin in 1 cup boiling water in bowl. Add pineapple and place in refrigerator until it thickens slightly.

- Fold in apples and pecans.

- Pour into solid mold or into 7 x 11-inch dish. Refrigerate until firm. Serves 8.

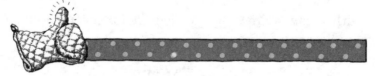

Gala apples originated in New Zealand and are a cross between Orange Pippin and Golden Delicious.

Blackberry-Blueberry Dream

1 (15 ounce) can crushed pineapple with liquid
1 (6 ounce) package blackberry gelatin
1 (15 ounce) can blueberries, drained

- Add enough water to pineapple liquid to make 2 cups. Put in saucepan and bring to a boil. Pour hot liquid over gelatin in bowl and mix until it dissolves.

- Refrigerate until mixture begins to thicken. Stir in pineapple and blueberries.

- Pour into 7 x 11-inch dish. Refrigerate.

Topping for Berry Dream Salad

1 (8 ounce) package cream cheese, softened
1 (8 ounce) carton sour cream
½ cup sugar
½ cup chopped pecans

- Beat cream cheese, sour cream and sugar in bowl until smooth and fluffy.

- Spoon over congealed salad. Sprinkle pecans over congealed salad. Refrigerate. Serves 8.

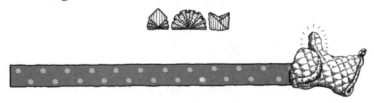

Shelled pecans may be stored in the refrigerator for up to 9 months. If frozen in sealed freezer bags, pecans may keep for up to 2 years. Unshelled pecans may be stored in an airtight container in a dry, cool place for up to 6 months.

Cherry Crush

1 (6 ounce) box cherry gelatin
1 (8 ounce) package cream cheese, softened
1 (20 ounce) can cherry pie filling
1 (15 ounce) can crushed pineapple with liquid

- Dissolve gelatin with ¾ cup boiling water in bowl.

- Add cream cheese and beat very slowly at first. Fold in pie filling and crushed pineapple.

- Pour into 9 x 13-inch baking dish. Refrigerate several hours before serving. Serves 8.

Creamy Cranberry Salad

1 (6 ounce) package cherry gelatin
1 (8 ounce) carton sour cream
1 (16 ounce) can whole cranberry sauce
1 (8 ounce) can crushed pineapple with liquid

- Dissolve gelatin in 1 cup boiling water in bowl and mix well.

- Stir in remaining ingredients and pour into 7 x 11-inch glass dish.

- Refrigerate until firm. Serves 8.

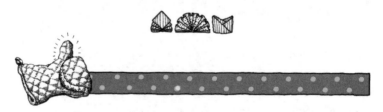

A great deal of what we see still depends on what we're looking for.

Nutty Grape-Pineapple Salad

1 pound seedless green grapes, halved
½ cup chopped pecans
1 (15 ounce) can pineapple tidbits, drained
½ cup mayonnaise

- Combine grapes, pecans and pineapple in bowl. Fold in mayonnaise. Serves 6.

Coconut-Orange Sampler

1 (6 ounce) package orange gelatin
1 (1 pint) carton vanilla ice cream, softened
½ cup flaked coconut
1 (11 ounce) can mandarin oranges, drained

- Dissolve gelatin in 1 cup boiling water in bowl and cool slightly. Fold in ice cream, coconut and oranges.

- Pour into 7 x 11-inch dish and freeze. Serves 8.

Crunchy Fruit Salad

2 red apples with peels, chopped
⅓ cup sunflower seeds
½ cup green grapes
⅓ cup vanilla yogurt

- Combine apples, sunflower seeds, grapes and yogurt in bowl. Stir to coat fruit with yogurt.

- Refrigerate before serving. Serves 4.

Stained-Glass Fruit Salad

2 (20 ounce) cans peach pie filling
3 bananas, sliced
1 (16 ounce) package frozen strawberries, drained
1 (20 ounce) can pineapple tidbits, drained

- Mix fruits in bowl, refrigerate and place in pretty crystal bowl.

- Refrigerate overnight. Serves 8 to 10.

Ranch-Style Cheeseburgers

1 (1 ounce) packet ranch salad dressing mix
1 pound lean ground beef
1 cup shredded cheddar cheese
4 large hamburger buns, toasted

- Combine dressing mix with beef and cheese in bowl. Shape into 4 patties.

- Cook on charcoal grill until they thoroughly cook and brown. Serve on hamburger buns. Serves 4.

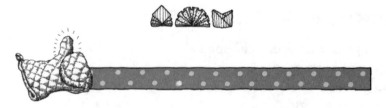

Cheese may be frozen. Processed cheeses will last 4 months frozen and cheddar or other natural cheeses will keep about 6 weeks when properly wrapped. Thaw all cheese overnight in refrigerator and use soon after thawing.

Pizza Burgers

1 pound lean ground beef
½ cup pizza sauce, divided
4 slices mozzarella cheese
Hamburger buns

- Combine beef, ½ teaspoon salt and ¼ cup pizza sauce in bowl.

- Mold into 4 patties and pan-fry over medium heat for 5 to 6 minutes on each side.

- Just before burgers are done, top each with 1 spoonful pizza sauce and 1 slice cheese.

- Serve on hamburger bun. Serves 4.

Hot Bunwiches

8 hamburger buns
8 slices Swiss cheese
8 slices ham
8 slices turkey

- Lay out all 8 buns. On bottom bun, place slices of Swiss cheese, ham and turkey.

- Place top bun over turkey. Wrap each bunwich individually in foil and place in freezer.

- When ready to serve, take out of freezer 2 to 3 hours before serving. Preheat oven to 325° and heat for about 30 minutes and serve hot. Serves 8.

TIP: *If you want it extra cheesy, add another slice of cheese, any kind.*

Cream Cheese Tea Sandwiches

1 (8 ounce) package cream cheese, softened
½ pound bacon, fried, finely chopped
12 - 14 slices whole wheat bread
1 (12 ounce) package bean sprouts

- Beat cream cheese in bowl until smooth. Add chopped bacon or chop cream cheese and bacon together in food processor.

- Spread bacon-cream cheese mixture on 6 to 8 slices bread. Add layer of bean sprouts and top with bread to make sandwiches.

- With sharp knife remove crust and cut each sandwich in 3 pieces. Refrigerate. Serves 6 to 8.

TIP: *If the cream cheese isn't creamy enough for you, add a little mayonnaise or butter.*

Italian Sausage Snacks

1 pound sweet Italian sausage, cooked, casing removed
1 red bell pepper, seeded, chopped
1 onion, chopped
1⅔ cups Italian-style spaghetti sauce

- Cook sausage, bell pepper and onion in skillet over medium heat until sausage browns and is no longer pink.

- Stir in spaghetti sauce and heat until boiling. Lower heat and simmer for 5 minutes and stir constantly. Serves 4.

TIP: *Sausage snacks are extra good served on hoagie rolls.*

Reuben's Buns

1 pound (8 count) package smoked frankfurters
8 hot dog buns
1 (8 ounce) can sauerkraut, well drained
Thousand Island dressing

- Preheat oven to 325°.

- Pierce each frankfurter and place into split buns.

- Arrange 2 tablespoons sauerkraut over each frank.

- Place in 9 x 13-inch shallow pan and drizzle with Thousand Island dressing.

- Heat in oven for about 15 minutes or until hot dogs are thoroughly hot. Serves 8.

Tasty Cream Cheese Sandwiches

2 (8 ounce) packages cream cheese, softened
1 (4 ounce) can black olives, chopped
¾ cups finely chopped pecans
Pumpernickel rye bread

- Beat cream cheese in bowl until creamy. Fold in olives and pecans.

- Trim crusts on bread. Spread cream cheese on bread.

- Slice sandwich into 3 finger strips. Yields 1½ cups.

Green Chile Grilled Cheese

4 slices American cheese
4 slices bread
1 (4 ounce) can diced green chilies, drained
3 tablespoons butter, softened

- Place 1 slice cheese on each of 2 slices bread. Sprinkle with green chilies.

- Top with 2 remaining slices cheese and remaining 2 slices bread. Butter outside of sandwiches.

- Brown sandwiches in large skillet over medium heat on both sides until golden brown and cheese melts. Serves 2.

Marshmallow Sandwiches

White bread or whole wheat bread
1 (7 ounce) jar marshmallow cream
Crunchy peanut butter
Butter

- On 1 slice bread, spread marshmallow cream. On second slice bread, spread peanut butter.

- Put marshmallow and peanut butter sides together. Eat sandwiches as is or brown sandwich in skillet with a little butter. Serves 6.

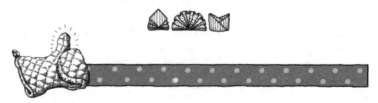

Happiness is a state of mind.
Anonymous

Vegetables
&
Side Dishes

Sesame Asparagus

6 fresh asparagus spears, trimmed
1 tablespoon butter
1 teaspoon lemon juice
1 teaspoon sesame seeds

- Place asparagus in skillet. Add ¼ cup water and bring to a boil. Reduce heat, cover and simmer for about 4 minutes.

- Melt butter in saucepan and add lemon juice and sesame seed.

- Drain asparagus and drizzle with butter mixture. Serves 2.

Creamy Asparagus Bake

2 (15 ounce) cans cut asparagus spears with liquid
3 eggs, hard-boiled, chopped
½ cup chopped pecans
1 (10 ounce) can cream of celery soup

- Preheat oven to 350°.

- Arrange asparagus spears in sprayed 2-quart baking dish. Top with eggs and pecans.

- Heat asparagus soup and add liquid from asparagus spears.

- Spoon over eggs and pecans. Cover and bake for 25 minutes. Serves 8.

My first desire for knowledge and my earliest passion for reading were awakened by my mother. Charles Dickens

Classic Baked Bean Stand-By

3 (15 ounce) cans baked beans
½ cup chili sauce
⅓ cup packed brown sugar
4 slices bacon, cooked, crumbled

- Preheat oven to 325°.

- Combine baked beans, chili sauce and brown sugar in sprayed 3-quart baking dish. Bake for 40 minutes.

- When ready to serve, sprinkle bacon on top. Serves 6.

Tasty Black-Eyed Peas

2 (10 ounce) packages frozen black-eyed peas
¾ cup chopped onion
3 tablespoons butter
1 (15 ounce) can Mexican stewed tomatoes with liquid

- Cook black-eyed peas according to package directions and drain.

- Saute green pepper and onion in butter in skillet. Add peas and tomatoes, cook over low heat until hot and stir often. Serves 8.

It's no secret that tomatoes are a critical part of our cooking. They are healthy and make many wonderful sauces. There are many varieties to choose from including whole, crushed, and diced. We recommend that you keep your shelves well stocked with plenty of canned tomatoes since many recipes include them.

Black-Eyed Peas and Okra

3 (15 ounce) cans black-eyed peas, drained
1 cup cooked, shredded ham
1 onion, chopped
1 pound small fresh whole okra pods

- Combine peas, ham and onion in large saucepan and bring to a boil.

- Place all okra on top of pea-onion mixture and do not stir.

- Bring to a boil again, lower heat and simmer for about 5 to 10 minutes or until okra is tender. Serve hot. Serves 8 to 10.

Easy Lemon Broccoli

1 (16 ounce) frozen package of broccoli florets
¼ cup (½ stick) butter
1 tablespoon lemon juice
½ teaspoon salt

- Cook broccoli according to package directions and drain.

- Melt butter in saucepan and stir in lemon juice and salt.

- Pour over broccoli and toss to coat. Serves 4.

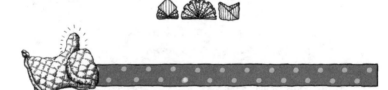

Two antennas met on a roof, fell in love and got married. The ceremony wasn't much, but the reception was excellent.

Shrimp-Almond Sauce with Broccoli

1 (16 ounce) package broccoli florets
1 (10 ounce) can cream of shrimp soup
1 (3 ounce) package cream cheese
⅓ cup slivered almonds, toasted

- Cook broccoli florets according to package directions.

- Combine shrimp soup and cream cheese in saucepan. Heat slowly until cream cheese melts and stir often.

- When ready to serve, pour over cooked broccoli and sprinkle almonds over top of sauce. Yields 1 cup sauce.

Cheddar-Broccoli Bake

1 (10 ounce) can cheddar cheese soup
½ cup milk
1 (16 ounce) bag frozen broccoli florets, cooked
1 (3 ounce) can french-fried onions

- Preheat oven to 350°.

- Mix soup, milk and broccoli in 2-quart baking dish. Bake for 25 minutes.

- Stir and sprinkle fried onions over broccoli mixture. Bake for additional 5 minutes or until onions are golden. Serves 6.

Nothing feels exactly like that moment during an argument when you realize you are wrong.

Creamy Vegetable Casserole

1 (16 ounce) package frozen broccoli, carrots and cauliflower
1 (10 ounce) can cream of mushroom soup
1 (8 ounce) carton garden-vegetable cream cheese
1 cup seasoned croutons

- Preheat oven to 350°.

- Cook vegetables according to package directions, drain and place in large bowl.

- Combine soup and cream cheese in saucepan and heat just enough to mix easily.

- Pour into vegetable mixture and mix well. Pour into 2-quart baking dish.

- Sprinkle with croutons. Bake for 25 minutes or until bubbly. Serves 6 to 8.

Tangy Carrot Coins

2 (15 ounce) cans sliced carrots, drained
2 tablespoons butter
2 tablespoons brown sugar
1 tablespoon dijon-style mustard

- Place all ingredients in saucepan. Cook and stir over medium heat for about 2 minutes. Serve hot. Serves 4 to 6.

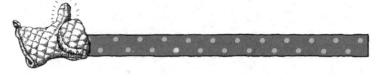

Less than six hours elapse from the time tomatoes are picked to the time they are processed and in a can.

Dilled Baby Carrots

1 (16 ounce) package fresh baby carrots
3 chicken bouillon cubes or 2 teaspoons bouillon granules
6 tablespoons (¾ stick) butter
2 teaspoons dill weed

- Boil carrots in water in saucepan with dissolved bouillon cubes until tender (about 8 minutes). Drain.

- Place in skillet with melted butter. Cook on low heat for only a few minutes and make sure butter coats all carrots.

- Sprinkle dill weed over carrots and shake to make sure dill is on all carrots.

- Place in serving dish and serve immediately. Serves 6.

Creamy Cabbage Bake

1 head cabbage, shredded
1 (10 ounce) can cream of celery soup
⅔ cup milk
1 (8 ounce) package shredded cheddar cheese

- Preheat oven to 325°.

- Place cabbage in sprayed 2-quart baking dish.

- Pour celery soup diluted with milk over top of cabbage. Cover and bake for 30 minutes.

- Uncover and sprinkle with cheese and bake for additional 5 minutes. Serves 6.

Fried Cabbage

1 small head cabbage, finely chopped
½ teaspoon salt
3 tablespoons olive oil
2 tablespoons Italian salad dressing

- Sprinkle cabbage with salt and set aside for 30 minutes.

- Heat oil in skillet until very hot. Add cabbage and stir-fry for about 5 minutes.

- Remove and add Italian dressing. Serves 6.

Italian Corn Mix

1 (16 ounce) package frozen whole kernel corn
2 slices bacon, cooked, crumbled
1 onion, chopped
1 (15 ounce) can Italian stewed tomatoes

- Combine all ingredients in 2-quart saucepan. Cook until most liquid in tomatoes cooks out and serve hot. Serves 6 to 8.

The staples of Indians who roamed Mexico and other parts of the New World were chile peppers, beans, corn and squash. From these basic ingredients, regional cuisines in Mexico and America developed into an art form.

Stuffed Corn Casserole

1 (15 ounce) can cream-style corn
1 (15 ounce) can whole kernel corn, drained
½ cup (1 stick) butter, melted
1 (6 ounce) package chicken stuffing mix

- Preheat oven to 350°.

- Combine all ingredients and ½ cup water in bowl and mix well.

- Spoon into sprayed 9 x 13-inch baking pan. Bake for 30 minutes. Serves 6.

Super Corn Casserole

2 (15 ounce) cans cream-style corn
½ cup (1 stick) butter, melted
1 (8 ounce) carton sour cream
1 (6 ounce) package jalapeno cornbread mix

- Preheat oven to 350°.

- Mix all ingredients and pour into sprayed 9 x 13-inch baking dish. Bake for 35 minutes. Serves 8 to 10.

The press must grow day in and day out – it is our Party's sharpest and most powerful weapon. Joseph Stalin

Wild West Corn

2 (15 ounce) cans whole kernel corn, drained
1 (10 ounce) can diced tomatoes and green chilies, drained
1 (8 ounce) package shredded Monterey Jack cheese
1 cup cheese cracker crumbs

- Preheat oven to 350°.

- Combine corn, tomatoes and green chilies, and cheese in large bowl and mix well.

- Pour into sprayed 2½-quart baking dish.

- Sprinkle cracker crumbs over casserole. Bake for 25 minutes. Serves 4 to 6.

Corn Pudding

1 (8 ounce) package corn muffin mix
1 (15 ounce) can cream-style corn
½ cup sour cream
3 eggs, slightly beaten

- Preheat oven to 350°.

- Combine all ingredients in bowl and pour into sprayed 2-quart baking dish.

- Bake for about 35 minutes. Serves 6.

No matter how old a mother is, she watches her middle-aged children for signs of improvement. Florida Scott-Maxwell

Cheesy Baked Eggplant

1 eggplant
½ cup mayonnaise
⅔ cup seasoned breadcrumbs
¼ cup grated parmesan cheese

- Preheat oven to 400°.

- Peel eggplant and slice ½-inch thick.

- Spread both sides with mayonnaise and dip in mixture of crumbs and parmesan. Coat both sides well.

- Place in single layer in shallow baking dish. Bake for 20 minutes. Serves 4.

Eggplant Casserole

1 large eggplant
1 cup cracker crumbs
1 cup shredded cheddar cheese, divided
1 (10 ounce) can diced tomatoes and green chilies

- Preheat oven to 350°.

- Peel and slice eggplant.

- Place eggplant in saucepan and cover with water. Cook for 10 minutes or until tender. Drain well on paper towels.

- Mash eggplant. Stir in cracker crumbs, ¾ cup cheese, and tomatoes and green chilies and mix well.

- Spoon eggplant mixture in sprayed 1-quart baking dish. Sprinkle with remaining cheese. Bake for 30 minutes. Serves 8.

Seasoned Green Beans

4 slices bacon, chopped
1 medium onion, chopped
2 (15 ounce) cans green beans, drained
1 teaspoon sugar

- Saute bacon and onion in skillet and drain.

- Add green beans and sugar and heat thoroughly. Serves 8.

Italian Green Beans

1 (16 ounce) package frozen Italian green beans
3 green onions with tops, chopped
2 tablespoons butter
1 teaspoon Italian seasoning

- Mix all ingredients plus ¼ cup water in 2-quart saucepan.

- Cook on medium-high heat for about 10 minutes or until beans are tender. Serves 6.

If you don't have a garlic press, put a clove between two pieces of plastic wrap and press the bottom of a glass to flatten the clove. You can also use a rubber mallet or flat side of a large knife. Mashing or pressing garlic releases more flavors than slicing or mincing.

Sesame Green Beans

1 pound fresh green beans
2 tablespoons soy sauce
¼ cup (½ stick) butter
½ cup toasted sesame seeds

- Cook green beans in medium saucepan until tender-crisp, about 10 minutes.

- Combine soy sauce and butter in saucepan. Cook over medium heat for a few minutes.

- Add to green beans and toss lightly. Add sesame seeds and toss again. Serves 4 to 6.

Crunchy Green Beans

3 (15 ounce) cans whole green beans
2 (10 ounce) cans cream of mushroom soup
2 (11 ounce) cans sliced water chestnuts, chopped, drained
2 (3 ounce) cans french-fried onions

- Preheat oven to 350°.

- Combine green beans, mushroom soup and water chestnuts in bowl.

- Pour mixture into sprayed 2-quart baking dish. Cover and bake for 30 minutes.

- Remove casserole from oven, sprinkle fried onions over top and bake for additional 10 minutes. Serves 8.

Cauliflower Winner

1 (16 ounce) package frozen cauliflower
1 (8 ounce) carton sour cream
1½ cups shredded American or cheddar cheese
4 teaspoons sesame seeds, toasted*

- Preheat oven to 350°.

- Cook cauliflower according to package directions.

- Drain and place half cauliflower in 2-quart baking dish. Spread half sour cream and half cheese, top with 2 teaspoons sesame seed and repeat layers.

- Bake for about 15 to 20 minutes. Serves 6.

*TIP: *Toasting brings out the flavor in nuts and seeds. Spread seeds on baking sheet and bake at 300° for 10 minutes.*

Spicy Hominy

2 (15 ounce) can yellow hominy, drained
1 (8 ounce) carton sour cream
1 (4 ounce) can diced green chilies
1¼ cups shredded cheddar cheese

- Preheat oven to 350°.

- Combine all ingredients and add a little salt in bowl. Pour into sprayed 1-quart baking dish and bake for about 20 minutes. Serves 4 to 6.

Fried Okra

Small, fresh garden okra
Milk or buttermilk
Cornmeal
2 - 3 tablespoons oil

- Thoroughly wash and drain okra. Cut off top and ends and slice.

- Toss okra with a little milk or buttermilk (just enough to make cornmeal stick). Sprinkle cornmeal over okra and toss.

- Heat oil in skillet. Fry okra and turn several times until okra is golden brown and crisp. Serves 4 ounces per person.

Cheesy Onion Casserole

5 sweet onions, sliced
½ cup (1 stick) butter
1 cup shredded cheddar cheese
22 saltine crackers, crushed

- Preheat oven to 325°.

- Saute onion in butter in skillet until soft.

- Layer half onions, half cheese, half crackers in sprayed 2-quart baking dish and repeat layers.

- Bake for 35 minutes. Serves 6.

I would rather try to carry 10 plastic grocery bags in each hand than make two trips to bring my groceries in.

Fast Parmesan Peas

2 (10 ounce) packages frozen green peas
3 tablespoons butter, melted
1 tablespoon lemon juice
⅓ cup grated parmesan cheese

- Microwave peas in 2 tablespoons water in bowl for 3 minutes.

- Rotate bowl half turn and cook for additional 3 minutes. Leave in oven for several minutes.

- Stir in butter, lemon juice and cheese. Microwave for additional 2 minutes. Serve hot. Serves 6.

Herbed Spinach

2 (16 ounce) packages frozen chopped spinach
1 (8 ounce) package cream cheese, softened
¼ cup (½ stick) butter, melted, divided
1 (6 ounce) package herbed-seasoned stuffing

- Preheat oven to 350°.

- Cook spinach according to package directions. Squeeze spinach between paper towels to completely remove excess moisture.

- Add cream cheese and half butter.

- Pour into sprayed baking dish. Spread herb stuffing on top and drizzle with remaining butter.

- Bake for 25 minutes. Serves 8.

Favorite Spinach Casserole

2 (10 ounce) packages frozen chopped spinach, thawed, well
    drained*
1 (1 ounce) packet onion soup mix
1 (8 ounce) carton sour cream
⅔ cup shredded Monterey Jack cheese

- Preheat oven to 350°.

- Combine spinach, onion soup mix and sour cream. Pour into
  sprayed 2-quart baking dish. Bake for 20 minutes.

- Take out of oven, sprinkle cheese over top and place casserole
  back in oven for 5 minutes. Serves 8.

*TIP: Squeeze spinach between paper towels to completely remove
    excess moisture.*

Ritzy Spinach Bake

2 (8 ounce) packages cream cheese, softened
1 (10 ounce) can cream of chicken soup
2 (16 ounce) packages frozen chopped spinach, thawed,
    well drained*
1 cup crushed round, buttery crackers

- Preheat oven to 325°.

- Beat cream cheese in bowl until smooth. Add soup and mix well.

- Stir in spinach. Spoon into sprayed 3-quart baking dish.

- Sprinkle cracker crumbs over top of casserole. Bake for
  35 minutes. Serves 8.

*TIP: Squeeze spinach between paper towels to completely remove
    excess moisture.*

Posh Squash

8 medium yellow squash, sliced
½ green bell pepper, seeded, chopped
1 small onion, chopped
1 (8 ounce) package shredded Mexican Velveeta® cheese

- Preheat oven to 350°.

- Combine squash, bell pepper and onion in large saucepan and just barely cover with water.

- Cook just until tender for about 10 to 15 minutes.

- Drain and add cheese. Stir until cheese melts and pour into sprayed 2-quart baking dish.

- Bake for 15 minutes. Serves 6 to 8.

Dynamite Squash Bake

5 medium yellow squash, sliced
2 potatoes, thinly sliced
1 onion, chopped
2 (10 ounce) cans cream of chicken soup

- Preheat oven to 350°.

- Layer squash, potatoes and onion in sprayed 2-quart baking dish.

- Combine soup and ¾ can water in saucepan and heat just enough to mix well. Pour over vegetables.

- Cover and bake for 45 minutes. Serves 8.

Baked Tomatoes with Basil

3 large tomatoes
1½ cups seasoned breadcrumbs
¼ cup (½ stick) butter, melted
Dried basil

- Preheat oven to 350°.

- Slice tomatoes in ½ to 1-inch thick slices and place on baking sheet.

- Sprinkle slices generously with breadcrumbs and top with butter and basil.

- Bake for 10 to 15 minutes or until light brown on top. Serves 6.

Southern-Fried Zucchini

3 large zucchini, grated
5 eggs
⅓ (12 ounce) box round buttery crackers, crushed
Oil

- Combine zucchini, eggs and cracker crumbs in bowl and mix well. Add cheese.

- Drop spoonfuls of mixture into skillet with a little oil. Fry for about 15 minutes and brown on each side. Serves 8.

TIP: *For an extra treat, add 1 cup grated parmesan cheese to mixture before browning.*

Walnut Zucchini

6 - 8 zucchini, julienned
½ red bell pepper, seeded, julienned
¼ cup (½ stick) butter
1 cup chopped walnuts

- Saute zucchini and bell pepper in butter in skillet until tender. Shake pan and toss zucchini to cook evenly. Pour off any excess butter.

- Add chopped walnuts. When walnuts blend and heat, serve immediately. Serves 6.

Potatoes Supreme

1 (32 ounce) package frozen hash-brown potatoes, thawed
1 onion, chopped
2 (10 ounce) cans cream of chicken soup
1 (8 ounce) carton sour cream

- Preheat oven to 350°.

- Combine potatoes, onion, soup and sour cream in large bowl. Pour into sprayed 9 x 13-inch baking dish.

- Cover and bake for 1 hour. Serves 8 to 10.

TIP: *When you have ½ cup shredded parmesan or cheddar cheese in your refrigerator, sprinkle it on top of the dish the last 5 minutes of baking. It changes up the recipe and you have a whole new dish.*

Potatoes with a Zip

1 (32 ounce) bag frozen hash-brown potatoes, thawed
1 (16 ounce) package cubed Velveeta® cheese
2 cups mayonnaise
1 (7 ounce) can diced green chilies

• Preheat oven to 325°.

• Combine hash browns, cheese, mayonnaise and green chilies in large bowl.

• Spoon into sprayed 9 x 13-inch baking dish. Cover and bake for 1 hour.

• Stir twice during baking to prevent burning. Serves 8 to 10.

Loaded Baked Potatoes

6 medium potatoes
1 (1 pound) package hot sausage
1 (16 ounce) package cubed Velveeta® cheese
1 (10 ounce) can diced tomatoes and green chilies, drained

• Preheat oven to 375°.

• Wrap potatoes in foil and bake for 1 hour or until done.

• Brown sausage in skillet and drain.

• Add cheese to sausage and heat until cheese melts. Add tomatoes and green chilies. Serve sausage-cheese mixture over baked potatoes. Serves 6.

Vegetable-Stuffed Potatoes

2 (10 ounce) cans fiesta nacho cheese soup
1 (16 ounce) bag frozen assorted vegetables, cooked, drained
8 large potatoes, baked
Pepper

- Heat soup and vegetables in saucepan.

- Cut lengthwise slice in top of each potato. Slightly mash flesh in each potato.

- Spoon sauce mixture on each potato. Sprinkle with a little pepper. Serves 8.

Easy Oven-Roasted Potatoes

2 pounds new (red) potatoes with peels
1 (1 ounce) packet onion soup mix
⅓ cup olive oil
½ teaspoon pepper

- Preheat oven to 425°.

- Wash potatoes and cut into bite-size pieces. Add all ingredients in large resealable bag. Shake until potatoes coat evenly.

- Empty coated potatoes into sprayed 9 x 13-inch baking pan.

- Bake, stirring twice, for 40 minutes or until golden brown. Serves 8.

Philly Potatoes

4½ cups instant mashed potatoes, prepared, hot
2 tablespoons freeze-dried chives
1 (8 ounce) package cream cheese, softened
1 egg, slightly beaten

- Preheat oven to 350°.

- Mix all ingredients in bowl and blend well. Place in sprayed 3-quart baking dish.

- Cover and bake for 30 minutes. Uncover and bake for additional 15 minutes. Serves 6.

Company Potatoes

5 potatoes, peeled, sliced
2 (8 ounce) cartons whipping cream
2 tablespoons dijon-style mustard
2 tablespoons butter

- Preheat oven to 350°.

- Layer potatoes in sprayed 9 x 13-inch baking dish.

- Combine cream, mustard and butter in saucepan and heat to boiling. Pour over potatoes.

- Cover and bake for 1 hour or until potatoes are tender. Serves 8.

Q: Why did the turkey cross the road?
A: To prove he wasn't chicken.

Cheddar Cheese Potatoes

1 (10 ounce) can cheddar cheese soup
⅓ cup sour cream
2 fresh green onions, chopped
3 cups prepared instant seasoned mashed potatoes

- Preheat oven to 350°.

- Heat soup in saucepan and add sour cream, onion and little pepper.

- Stir in potatoes until they blend well. Pour into sprayed 2-quart baking dish. Bake for 25 minutes. Serves 6.

Ranch-Style Mashed Potatoes

4 cups prepared instant mashed potatoes
1 (1 ounce) packet ranch salad dressing mix
¼ cup (½ stick) butter
½ cup sour cream

- Combine all ingredients in saucepan.

- Heat on low until potatoes are hot. Serves 8.

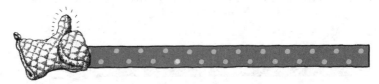

Good vegetable sources of vitamin C include tomatoes, peppers, broccoli and cauliflower.

Potato Puff

3 eggs, separated
2 cups prepared instant mashed potatoes
½ cup sour cream
2 teaspoons dried parsley

- Preheat oven to 350°.

- Beat egg whites in bowl until stiff but still moist and set aside.

- In separate bowl, beat yolks until smooth and add to potato mixture.

- Fold in beaten egg whites, sour cream and parsley.

- Pour into sprayed 2-quart baking dish. Bake for 45 minutes. Serves 6.

Grilled New Potatoes

1 pound new (red) potatoes, halved
3 tablespoons orange marmalade
1 teaspoon brown sugar
2 tablespoons butter, melted

- Cook new potatoes in medium saucepan covered in boiling water until tender-crisp.

- Drain and thread on skewers. Combine marmalade, brown sugar and butter and brush mixture over potatoes.

- Grill over medium hot coals until potatoes are brown, about 5 minutes on each side. Baste frequently. Serves 6.

Potato Souffle

2⅔ cups instant mashed potatoes
2 eggs, beaten
1 cup shredded cheddar cheese
1 (3 ounce) can french-fried onions

- Preheat oven to 325°.

- Prepare mashed potato mix according to package directions. Add eggs, cheese and stir until they blend well.

- Spoon mixture into lightly sprayed 2-quart dish. Sprinkle with fried onions.

- Bake for 25 minutes. Serves 6.

Potato Pancakes

3 pounds white potatoes, peeled, grated
1 onion, finely minced
3 eggs, beaten
½ cup seasoned dry breadcrumbs

- Combine potatoes, onions, eggs and breadcrumbs in large bowl and mix well.

- Drop spoonfuls of mixture in skillet in hot oil and brown on both sides. Serves 8.

TIP: Use a little oil in skillet.

Ham Baked Potatoes

4 potatoes, baked
1 cup cooked, diced ham
1 (10 ounce) can cream of mushroom soup
1 cup shredded cheddar cheese

- Place hot potatoes in microwave-safe plate. Cut in half lengthwise.

- Fluff up potatoes with fork. Top each potato with one-fourth ham.

- Heat soup with ¼ cup water in saucepan and heat just until spreadable.

- Spoon soup over potatoes and top with cheese. Microwave on HIGH for 4 minutes or until hot. Serves 4.

 ## Broccoli-Topped Potatoes

4 hot baked potatoes, halved
1 cup cooked, diced ham
1 (10 ounce) can cream of broccoli soup
½ cup shredded cheddar cheese

- Place hot baked potatoes on microwave-safe plate.

- Carefully fluff up potatoes with fork. Top each potato with ham.

- Stir soup in can until smooth. Spoon soup over potatoes and top with cheese.

- Microwave on HIGH for 4 minutes. Serves 4.

Whipped Sweet Potatoes

2 (15 ounce) cans sweet potatoes
¼ cup (½ stick) butter, melted
¼ cup orange juice
1 cup miniature marshmallows

- Preheat oven to 350°.

- Combine sweet potatoes, butter and orange juice in bowl.

- Beat until fluffy. Fold in marshmallows. Spoon into sprayed
  2-quart baking dish. Bake for 25 minutes. Serves 8.

Sweet Potato Casserole

1 (28 ounce) can sweet potatoes, drained
½ cup chopped pecans
1½ cups packed light brown sugar
½ cup (1 stick) butter, melted

- Preheat oven to 350°.

- Slice sweet potatoes into 2-quart baking dish. Sprinkle pecans
  over sweet potatoes.

- Make syrup of brown sugar and butter with just enough water
  to make it thin enough to pour in saucepan. Bring to a boil and
  pour syrup over sweet potatoes.

- Bake for 30 minutes or until potatoes brown. Serves 4 to 6.

Tasty Rice Bake

1½ cups rice
½ cup (1 stick) butter, melted
1 (10 ounce) can French onion soup
1 (8 ounce) can sliced water chestnuts, drained, chopped

• Preheat oven to 350°.

• Combine rice, butter, soup, water chestnuts and 1¼ cups water.

• Pour into sprayed 2-quart baking dish. Cover and bake for 1 hour. Serves 6.

Creamy Baked Rice

2 cups rice
½ cup (1 stick) butter, melted
1 (10 ounce) can cream of celery soup
1 (10 ounce) can cream of onion soup

• Preheat oven to 350°.

• Combine rice, butter, soups and 1½ cups water. Pour into sprayed 3-quart baking dish. Bake for 1 hour. Serves 8.

The sweet potato is one of the most nutritious vegetables. Fat free and cholesterol free, it is full of fiber and has significant amounts of vitamins C and E. It can be baked, grilled, sauteed, fried, boiled, steamed and eaten raw in a variety of dishes - even desserts.

Easy Rice

1 onion, finely chopped
2 tablespoons butter
1 cup white rice
2 (14 ounce) cans chicken broth

• Preheat oven to 350°.

• Saute onion in butter until transparent.

• Combine onion, rice and broth in 2-quart baking dish. Cover and bake for 55 minutes. Serves 8.

Tasty Rice Bowl

¼ cup (½ stick) butter
1 cup white rice
2 (15 ounce) cans beef broth
¼ cup grated parmesan cheese

• Preheat oven to 350°.

• Melt butter in 3-quart baking dish. Add rice and pour beef broth over rice.

• Sprinkle with parmesan cheese. Cover and bake for 45 minutes. Serves 4 to 6.

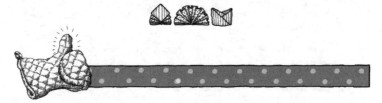

Tomatoes for processing are picked ripe and red. Fresh market tomatoes are picked green.

Seasoned Brown Rice

1 cup rice
1 (10 ounce) can French onion soup
1 (10 ounce) can beef broth
3 tablespoons butter, melted

- Preheat oven to 350°.

- Place rice in sprayed 2-quart baking dish. Combine soup, broth and butter in bowl. Pour over rice.

- Cover and bake for 45 minutes. Serves 4 to 6.

Delicioso Spanish Rice

6 tablespoons (¾ stick) butter, melted
1 onion, chopped
2 cups cooked rice
1 (10 ounce) can diced tomatoes and green chilies

- Preheat oven to 350°.

- Combine butter, onion, rice, and tomatoes and green chilies in large bowl.

- Spoon mixture into sprayed 3-quart baking dish. Cover and bake for 30 minutes. Serves 8.

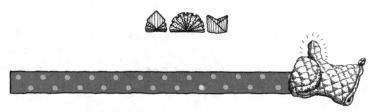

Deja moo... the feeling that you've heard this bull before.

Spinach Fettuccini Toss

1 (6 ounce) can tomato paste
1 (5 ounce) can evaporated milk
½ cup (1 stick) butter
1 (12 ounce) package spinach fettuccini

- Combine tomato paste, evaporated milk and butter in saucepan and cook until butter melts.

- Cook fettuccini according to package directions and place in serving bowl. Serve sauce over fettuccini. Serves 6.

Creamy Fettuccini

1 (8 ounce) package fettuccini
1 pound Italian sausage
1 (10 ounce) can cream of mushroom soup
1 (16 ounce) carton sour cream

- Preheat oven to 325°.

- Cook fettuccini according to package directions and drain.

- Cut sausage into 1-inch pieces, brown in skillet over medium heat and cook for about 8 minutes. Drain.

- Mix all ingredients in bowl and place in sprayed 2-quart baking dish.

- Cover and bake for 30 minutes. Serves 6.

Creamy Pasta Side

1 (8 ounce) jar roasted red peppers, drained
1 (14 ounce) can chicken broth
1 (3 ounce) package cream cheese
1 (8 ounce) package favorite pasta, cooked

- Combine red peppers and broth in blender and mix well. Pour into saucepan and heat to boiling.

- Turn heat down and whisk in cream cheese, mixing until cream cheese melts. Serve over your favorite pasta. Serves 6.

Special Macaroni and Cheese

1 (8 ounce) package small macaroni shells
1 (15 ounce) can stewed tomatoes
1 (8 ounce) package cubed Velveeta® cheese
3 tablespoons butter, melted

- Preheat oven to 350°.

- Cook shells according to package directions in saucepan and drain.

- Combine shells, tomatoes, cheese cubes and butter in large bowl.

- Pour into sprayed 2-quart baking dish. Cover and bake for 35 minutes. Serves 6 to 8.

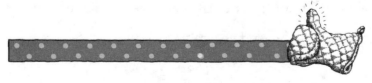

Pasta needs a lot of water to cook properly. Use at least two quarts for every eight ounces of dried pasta.

Three-Cheese Macaroni

1 cup macaroni
1½ cups small curd cottage cheese, drained
1½ cups shredded cheddar or American cheese
¼ cup grated parmesan cheese

- Preheat oven to 350°.

- Cook macaroni according to package directions in saucepan and drain.

- Combine cottage cheese and cheeses in bowl. Add macaroni to cheese mixture.

- Spoon into sprayed 2-quart baking dish. Cover and bake for 35 minutes. Serves 4 to 6.

Carnival Couscous

1 (6 ounce) box herbed-chicken couscous
¼ cup (½ stick) butter
1 red bell pepper, diced
1 yellow squash, diced

- Cook couscous according to package directions in saucepan, but leave out butter.

- With butter in saucepan, saute bell pepper and squash and cook for about 10 minutes or until vegetables are almost tender.

- Combine couscous and vegetables. Serve hot. Serves 8.

Main Dishes

Chicken Delight

6 boneless, skinless chicken breast halves
1 (8 ounce) carton whipped cream cheese with onion and chives
Butter, softened
6 bacon strips

- Preheat oven to 375°.

- Flatten chicken to ½-inch thickness. Spread 3 tablespoons cream cheese over each.

- Dot with butter and roll. Wrap each with bacon strip.

- Place seam-side down in sprayed 9 x 13-inch baking dish.

- Bake for 40 to 45 minutes or until juices run clear.

- To brown, broil 6 inches from heat for about 3 minutes or until bacon is crisp. Serves 6.

Saucy Chicken

5 - 6 boneless, skinless chicken breast halves
2 cups thick-and-chunky salsa
⅓ cup packed light brown sugar
1½ tablespoons dijon-style mustard

- Preheat oven to 350°.

- Place chicken breasts in sprayed 9 x 13-inch baking dish.

- Combine salsa, brown sugar and mustard in bowl and pour over chicken.

- Cover and bake for 45 minutes. Serves 6.

TIP: This tastes great served over cooked rice.

Golden Chicken

6 boneless, skinless chicken breast halves
¼ cup (½ stick) butter
1(10 ounce) can golden mushroom soup
½ cup sliced almonds

- Preheat oven to 350°.

- Place chicken breasts in sprayed 9 x 13-inch baking pan.

- Combine butter, soup, almonds and ¼ cup water in saucepan. Heat and mix just until butter melts.

- Pour mixture over chicken. Cover and bake for 1 hour. Serves 6.

Chicken Crunch

4 - 6 boneless, skinless chicken breast halves
½ cup Italian salad dressing
½ cup sour cream
2½ cups crushed corn flakes

- Place chicken in resealable plastic bag and add salad dressing and sour cream. Seal and refrigerate for 1 hour.

- When ready to bake, preheat oven to 375°.

- Remove chicken from marinade and discard marinade.

- Dredge chicken in corn flakes and place in sprayed 9 x 13-inch baking dish.

- Bake for 45 minutes. Serves 6.

Catalina Chicken

6 - 8 boneless, skinless chicken breast halves
1 (8 ounce) bottle Catalina dressing
1½ cups crushed cracker crumbs
1 teaspoon pepper

- Marinate chicken breasts in Catalina dressing for 3 to 4 hours and discard marinade.

- When ready to bake, preheat oven to 350°.

- Combine pepper and cracker crumbs in bowl.

- Dip each chicken breast in crumbs and place in sprayed 10 x 15-inch baking dish.

- Bake for 1 hour. Serves 6.

Cola Chicken

4 - 6 boneless, skinless chicken breast halves
1 cup ketchup
1 cup cola
2 tablespoons Worcestershire sauce

- Preheat oven to 350°.

- Place chicken in 9 x 13-inch baking dish.

- Mix ketchup, cola and Worcestershire sauce in bowl and pour over chicken. Cover and bake for 50 minutes. Serves 6.

Asparagus Chicken

1 (1 ounce) packet hollandaise sauce mix
2 large boneless, skinless chicken breasts, cut into strips
1 (15 ounce) can asparagus spears
1 (8 ounce) package wide noodles

- Prepare hollandaise sauce according to package directions.

- Cook chicken strips in large skillet for 12 to 15 minutes or until brown and stir occasionally. Add hollandaise sauce and lemon juice.

- Cover and cook for additional 10 minutes and stir occasionally.

- When ready to serve, place chicken strips over noodles and top with heated asparagus spears. Serves 6.

Peachy Chicken

½ cup Italian dressing
2 teaspoons ground ginger
4 boneless, skinless chicken breast halves
½ cup peach preserves

- Combine Italian dressing and ginger in large resealable plastic bag.

- Place chicken in bag and turn several times to coat chicken. Place in refrigerator, turn occasionally and marinate 4 hours or overnight.

- When ready to cook, remove chicken.

- Broil chicken in oven until it is no longer pink and brush with preserves last 5 minutes of cooking. Serves 4.

Mushroom Chicken with Wine

6 - 8 boneless, skinless chicken breast halves
1 (10 ounce) can cream of mushroom soup
1 (10 ounce) can cream of onion soup
1 cup white wine

- Preheat oven to 325°.

- Brown chicken in sprayed skillet. Place in 10 x 15-inch baking dish.

- Combine soups and wine in bowl and pour over chicken.

- Cover and bake for 35 minutes. Uncover and bake for additional 25 minutes. Serves 8.

Baked Chicken Supreme

6 boneless, skinless chicken breast halves
½ cup (1 stick) butter, melted
1 (6 ounce) box cornbread stuffing mix with seasoning, crushed

- Preheat oven to 350°.

- Dip chicken breast in melted butter. Roll in cornbread stuffing mix to coat. Place in baking dish.

- Bake for 45 minutes. Serves 6.

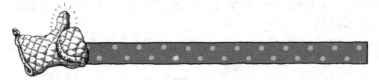

Q: What do you get if you cross a
chicken with a cement mixer?
A: A bricklayer.

Pineapple-Glazed Chicken

4 boneless, skinless chicken breast halves, cubed
1 (15 ounce) can pineapple chunks with juice
½ cup honey mustard grill-and-glaze sauce
1 red bell pepper, seeded, chopped

- Brown chicken in skillet and cook on low heat for 15 minutes. Add pineapple, honey mustard and bell pepper.

- Bring to a boil, reduce heat to low and simmer for 10 to 15 minutes or until sauce thickens slightly. Serves 4.

TIP: This chicken is wonderful over cooked rice.

Rosemary Chicken

½ cup flour
1 tablespoon dried rosemary, divided
Italian dressing
3 - 5 boneless, skinless chicken breast halves

- Preheat oven to 350°.

- Combine flour and half rosemary in bowl. In separate shallow bowl, pour a little Italian dressing and dip chicken breasts in dressing.

- Dredge chicken in flour mixture. Place in sprayed 9 x 13-inch shallow baking dish.

- Bake for 40 minutes. Remove from oven and sprinkle remaining rosemary over breasts and cook for an additional 10 minutes. Serves 3 to 5.

Chicken Dipsticks

1½ cups cornbread stuffing mix
4 tablespoons olive oil
4 boneless, skinless chicken breast halves
Chicken Dipsticks Sauce

- Preheat oven to 350°.

- Place stuffing mix in resealable plastic bag and crush with rolling pin.

- Add oil to center of 9 x 13-inch baking pan and spread around entire pan.

- Cut chicken breasts into 3 or 4 pieces, dip in stuffing mix and place in baking pan. Arrange chicken making sure pieces are not touching.

- Bake for 25 minutes. Remove from oven, turn pieces over and bake for additional 15 minutes or until brown. Serves 4.

Chicken Dipsticks Sauce

¼ cup honey
3 tablespoons spicy brown mustard

- Combine honey and brown mustard in bowl. Serve chicken with sauce and enjoy. Yields ⅓ cup.

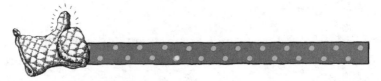

Reduced-sodium, reduced-fat chicken broth works just as well as chicken broth and helps lower one's sodium intake.

Lemonade Chicken

6 boneless, skinless chicken breast halves
1 (6 ounce) can frozen lemonade concentrate, thawed
⅓ cup soy sauce
1 teaspoon garlic powder

- Preheat oven to 350°.

- Place chicken in sprayed 9 x 13-inch baking dish.

- Combine lemonade concentrate, soy sauce and garlic powder in bowl and pour over chicken.

- Cover and bake for 45 minutes. Uncover, pour juices over chicken and cook for additional 10 minutes. Serves 6.

Classy Chicken

4 boneless, skinless chicken breast halves
¼ cup lime juice
1 (1 ounce) packet Italian salad dressing mix
¼ cup (½ stick) butter, melted

- Preheat oven to 325°.

- Place chicken in shallow baking dish.

- Mix lime juice, salad dressing mix and melted butter in bowl and pour over chicken.

- Cover and bake for 1 hour. Remove cover for last 15 minutes of cooking time. Serves 4.

Mozzarella Cutlets

4 boneless, skinless chicken breast halves
1 cup Italian seasoned dry breadcrumbs, divided
1 cup prepared spaghetti sauce
4 slices mozzarella cheese

- Preheat oven to 350°.

- Pound each chicken breast to flatten slightly.

- Coat chicken well in breadcrumbs. Arrange chicken breasts in sprayed 9 x 13-inch baking dish.

- Place quarter of sauce over each portion. Place 1 slice cheese over each and garnish with remaining breadcrumbs.

- Bake for 45 minutes. Serves 4.

Crispy Nutty Chicken

⅓ cup minced dry roasted peanuts
1 cup corn flake crumbs
½ cup ranch buttermilk salad dressing
5 - 6 chicken breast halves

- Preheat oven to 350°.

- Combine peanuts and corn flake crumbs on wax paper. Pour salad dressing into pie pan.

- Dip each piece chicken in salad dressing and roll in crumb mixture to coat.

- Arrange chicken in sprayed 9 x 13-inch shallow baking dish.

- Bake for 50 minutes until light brown. Serves 5 to 6.

Sunday Chicken

5 - 6 boneless, skinless chicken breast halves
½ cup sour cream
¼ cup soy sauce
1 (10 ounce) can French onion soup

- Preheat oven to 350º.

- Place chicken in sprayed 9 x 13-inch baking dish.

- Combine sour cream, soy sauce and soup in saucepan and heat just enough to mix well. Pour over chicken breasts.

- Cover and bake for 55 minutes. Serves 5 to 6.

Bacon-Wrapped Chicken

1 (4 ounce) jar sliced dried beef, separated
6 strips bacon
6 boneless, skinless chicken breast halves
1 (10 ounce) can cream of chicken soup

- Preheat oven to 325º.

- Place dried beef in sprayed 9 x 13-inch baking dish. Wrap bacon strip around each chicken breast half and place over beef.

- Heat soup and ¼ cup water in saucepan and pour over chicken.

- Cover and bake for 1 hour 10 minutes. Serves 6.

The longest recorded flight of a chicken is 13 seconds.

Marinated Garlic Chicken

4 - 5 boneless, skinless chicken breast halves
1 tablespoon oregano
¾ teaspoon garlic powder
½ cup (1 stick) butter, melted

- Place chicken breasts in resealable plastic bag and add oregano, garlic powder and butter. Marinate in refrigerator for 3 or 4 hours.

- When ready to bake, preheat oven to 325°.

- Place drained chicken in shallow baking dish. Cover and bake for 1 hour. Serves 4 to 5.

Ritzy Chicken Surprise

⅓ (12 ounce) box round buttery crackers, crushed
¼ teaspoon pepper
6 boneless, skinless chicken breast halves
½ cup sour cream

- Preheat oven to 350°.

- Combine cracker crumbs and pepper. Dip chicken in sour cream and roll in cracker crumbs mixture.

- Place chicken in sprayed shallow baking dish. Bake for 55 minutes. Serves 6.

Jiffy Chicken

6 boneless, skinless chicken breast halves
¾ cup mayonnaise
2 cups crushed corn flake crumbs
½ cup grated parmesan cheese

• Preheat oven to 325°.

• Dip chicken in mayonnaise and spread mayonnaise over chicken
with brush.

• Combine corn flakes and parmesan cheese in bowl. Dip
mayonnaise-covered chicken in corn flake mixture. Get plenty
of crumbs on chicken.

• Place in sprayed 9 x 13-inch glass baking dish. Bake for 1 hour.
Serves 6.

Skillet Chicken and Stuffing

1 (6 ounce) box stuffing mix for chicken
1 (16 ounce) package frozen whole kernel corn
¼ cup (½ stick) butter
4 boneless, skinless chicken breast halves, cooked

• Combine contents of seasoning packet in stuffing mix, corn,
1⅔ cups water and butter in large skillet.

• Bring to a boil. Reduce heat, cover and simmer for 5 minutes.

• Stir in stuffing mix just until moist. Cut chicken into thin slices.
Mix with stuffing-corn mixture.

• Cook on low heat just until thoroughly hot. Serves 4.

Chicken Curry

2 (10 ounce) cans cream of mushroom soup
2 teaspoons curry powder
⅓ cup chopped slivered almonds, toasted
4 boneless, skinless chicken breast halves, cooked, cubed

- Combine soup, 1 soup can water, curry powder, almonds and cubed chicken in large saucepan.

- Heat and cook for 5 minutes and stir frequently. Serves 4.

TIP: This chicken is exceptional when served over white rice.

Oven-Glazed Chicken

4 boneless, skinless chicken breast halves
1 (10 ounce) can Italian tomato soup
2 tablespoons marinade for chicken
2 tablespoons packed brown sugar

- Preheat oven to 350°.

- Place chicken breasts in sprayed 7 x 11-inch baking dish.

- Combine tomato soup, marinade for chicken and brown sugar in small bowl and mix well. Spoon over chicken.

- Bake for 1 hour. Serves 4.

If a rooster is not present in a flock of hens, a hen will often take the role, stop laying and begin to crow.

Apricot-Ginger Chicken

2 teaspoons ground ginger
¾ cup Italian dressing
4 boneless, skinless chicken breast halves
⅔ cup apricot preserves

- Combine ginger and Italian dressing; set aside ¼ cup. Place remaining dressing in large resealable plastic bag.

- Add chicken to bag and marinate in refrigerator overnight; turn occasionally.

- When ready to bake, preheat oven to 350°.

- When ready to cook, remove chicken and place in sprayed 9 x 13-inch baking dish.

- Pour ¼ cup marinade in saucepan, bring to a boil and cook for 1 minute. Remove from heat, stir in preserves and set aside.

- Bake chicken for 45 minutes and brush with cooked marinade mixture last 10 minutes of cooking. Serves 4.

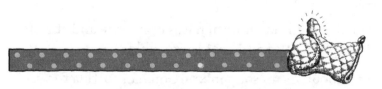

According to lore, Chicken, Alaska got its name because the locals wanted to honor the state bird, the Ptarmigan, by naming their town Ptarmigan, Alaska. But they couldn't spell Ptarmigan. However, they could spell chicken.

Quick-Fix Chicken Supper

5 boneless, skinless chicken breast halves
5 slices onion
5 potatoes, peeled, quartered
1(10 ounce) can cream of celery soup

- Preheat oven to 325°.

- Place chicken breasts in sprayed 9 x 13-inch baking dish. Top chicken with onion slices and place potatoes around chicken.

- Heat soup with ¼ cup water in saucepan just enough to pour soup over chicken and vegetables.

- Cover and bake for 1 hour 10 minutes. Serves 5.

Chicken Quesadillas

3 boneless, skinless chicken breast halves, cubed
1 (10 ounce) can cheddar cheese soup
⅔ cup chunky salsa
10 flour tortillas

- Preheat oven to 400°.

- Cook chicken in skillet until juices evaporate and stir often. Add soup and salsa and heat thoroughly.

- Spread about ⅓ cup soup mixture on half tortilla to within ½-inch of edge.

- Moisten edge with water, fold over and seal. Place tortillas on 2 baking sheets.

- Bake for 5 to 6 minutes. Serves 6 to 10.

Chicken Oriental

1 (10 ounce) jar sweet-and-sour sauce
1 (1 ounce) packet onion soup mix
1 (16 ounce) can whole cranberry sauce
6 - 8 boneless, skinless chicken breast halves

- Preheat oven to 325°.

- Combine sweet-and-sour sauce, onion soup mix and cranberry sauce in bowl.

- Place chicken breasts in sprayed 10 x 15-inch shallow baking dish. Pour cranberry mixture over chicken breasts.

- Cover and bake for 30 minutes. Uncover and bake for additional 25 minutes. Serves 6 to 8.

Fried Chicken Breasts

4 boneless, skinless chicken breast halves
2 eggs, beaten
20 saltine crackers, crushed
Oil

- Pound chicken breasts to ¼-inch thickness.

- Combine eggs, a little pepper and 2 tablespoons water in bowl.

- Dip chicken in egg mixture and crushed crackers and coat well. Deep fry until golden brown and drain well. Serves 4.

One-Dish Chicken Bake

1 (6 ounce) package chicken stuffing mix
4 boneless, skinless chicken breast halves
1 (10 ounce) can cream of mushroom soup
½ cup sour cream

- Preheat oven to 375°.

- Toss stuffing mix and 1⅔ cups water in bowl and set aside.

- Place chicken in sprayed 9 x 13-inch baking dish.

- Mix soup and sour cream in saucepan and heat just enough to pour over chicken. Spoon stuffing evenly over top. Bake for 40 minutes. Serves 4.

Sweet 'n Spicy Chicken

1 pound boneless, skinless chicken breast halves, cubed
3 tablespoons taco seasoning
1 (11 ounce) jar chunky salsa
1 cup peach preserves

- Place chicken in large resealable plastic bag, add taco seasoning and toss to coat.

- Brown chicken in skillet. Combine salsa and preserves in bowl. Stir into skillet.

- Bring to a boil. Reduce heat, cover and simmer for 30 minutes or until juices run clear. Serves 4.

TIP: Try serving this over cooked rice or noodles. It's great.

Tempting Chicken

3 boneless, skinless chicken breast halves
3 boneless, skinless chicken thighs
1 (16 ounce) jar tomato-alfredo sauce
1 (10 ounce) can tomato bisque soup

• Brown chicken pieces in large skillet.

• Combine tomato-alfredo sauce, tomato bisque soup and ½ cup water in bowl and pour over chicken pieces.

• Cover and simmer for about 30 minutes. Serves 6.

Italian Chicken and Rice

3 boneless, chicken breast halves, cut into strips
1 (14 ounce) can chicken broth seasoned with Italian herbs
¾ cup rice
¼ cup grated parmesan cheese

• Cook chicken in non-stick skillet until brown and stir often. Remove chicken and set aside.

• Add broth and rice to skillet. Heat to boiling point. Cover and simmer over low heat for 25 minutes. (Check to see if rice needs more water.)

• Stir in parmesan cheese. Return chicken to skillet. Cover and cook for 5 minutes or until done. Serves 3 to 4.

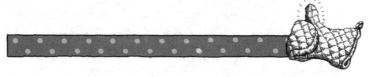

In Gainesville, Georgia - the chicken capital of the world - it's illegal to eat chicken with a fork.

El Pronto Chicken

4 boneless, skinless chicken breast halves
½ cup (1 stick) butter, melted
⅔ cup seasoned breadcrumbs
½ cup grated parmesan cheese

• Preheat oven to 350°.

• Dip chicken in butter. Mix breadcrumbs and parmesan cheese in bowl.

• Roll chicken in crumb-cheese mixture. Place in sprayed 9 x 13-inch baking dish.

• Cover and bake for 55 minutes. Serves 4.

TIP: *Cooked rice is always a complementary addition to chicken. Try serving this dish over cooked rice.*

Peanut oil is considered one of the best oils for frying because it has a very high smoke point. The oil can reach higher temperatures than most oils before it begins to smoke. Peanut oil does not absorb or transfer flavors, so the same oil is used for different foods without it affecting the taste of the foods.

EZ Chicken

6 boneless, skinless chicken breast halves
1 (10 ounce) can cream of chicken soup
1 (3 ounce) package cream cheese
1 (8 ounce) carton sour cream

- Preheat oven to 300°.

- Place chicken breasts in sprayed shallow 9 x 13-inch baking dish.

- Combine soup, cream cheese and sour cream in saucepan. Heat on low just until cream cheese melts and mixes well.

- Pour mixture over chicken breasts, cover and bake for 1 hour. Uncover and bake for additional 15 minutes. Serves 6.

TIP: *Check your pantry and sprinkle your favorite seasonings on the chicken before baking. Lemon pepper is always a good choice with chicken.*

Sesame Chicken

½ cup (1 stick) butter, melted
¾ tablespoon chili powder
4 boneless, skinless chicken breast halves
1 cup sesame seeds, lightly toasted

- Preheat oven to 325°.

- Combine butter and chili powder in bowl.

- Dip chicken in butter mixture and roll in sesame seeds.

- Place in sprayed 9 x 13- inch baking dish. Bake for 1 hour and turn after 30 minutes. Serves 4.

Honey-Mustard Chicken

⅓ cup dijon-style mustard
½ cup honey
1 tablespoon dried dill
2½ pounds chicken quarters, skinned

- Preheat oven to 350°.

- Combine mustard, honey and dill in bowl. Arrange chicken quarters in 10 x 15-inch baking dish.

- Pour mustard mixture over chicken. Turn chicken over and make sure mustard mixture coats chicken.

- Cover and bake for 35 minutes. Uncover and bake for additional 10 minutes. Serves 4.

Nacho Chicken

8 chicken quarters
2 (10 ounce) cans fiesta nacho cheese soup
¾ cup milk
3 tablespoons marinade for chicken

- Preheat oven to 350°.

- Place chicken quarters in sprayed 10 x 15-inch baking pan with sides.

- Combine soup, milk and marinade for chicken in saucepan and spread over chicken.

- Cover and bake for 1 hour. Serves 8.

Sunshine Chicken

4 chicken quarters
1 cup flour
1 cup barbecue sauce
½ cup orange juice

- Preheat oven to 350°.

- Place chicken in bowl of flour and coat well.

- Brown chicken in skillet and place in sprayed shallow baking pan.

- Combine barbecue sauce and orange juice in bowl. Pour over chicken.

- Cover and bake for 45 minutes. Remove from oven, spoon sauce over chicken and bake uncovered for additional 20 minutes. Serves 4.

Company Chicken

8 chicken quarters
2 (10 ounce) cans cream of mushroom soup
1 (1 pint) carton sour cream
1 cup sherry

- Preheat oven to 300°.

- Place chickens in large shallow baking dish.

- Combine soup, sour cream and sherry in saucepan over low to medium heat for 5 minutes. Pour mixture over chicken.

- Cover and bake for 1 hour 15 minutes. Serves 8.

TIP: This is great served over cooked rice.

Sweet-and-Sour Chicken

2 - 3 pounds chicken pieces
Olive oil
1 (1 ounce) packet onion soup mix
1 (6 ounce) can frozen orange juice concentrate, thawed

- Preheat oven to 350°.

- Brown chicken in little oil in skillet. Place in sprayed 10 x 15-inch baking dish.

- Combine onion soup mix, orange juice and ⅔ cup water in small bowl and stir well. Pour over chicken.

- Bake for 50 minutes. Serves 8 to 10.

Adobe Chicken

2 cups cooked brown rice
1 (10 ounce) can diced tomatoes and green chilies
3 cups cooked, chopped chicken
2 (8 ounce) package shredded Monterey Jack cheese, divided

- Preheat oven to 325°.

- Combine rice, tomatoes and green chilies, chicken, and half Jack cheese.

- Spoon into sprayed 7 x 11-inch baking dish. Cover and bake for 30 minutes.

- Sprinkle remaining cheese over casserole and bake uncovered for 5 minutes. Serves 4 to 6.

Noon-Time Chicken Special

4 thick cooked chicken breast slices
1 (3 ounce) package cream cheese, softened
3 tablespoons salsa
2 tablespoons mayonnaise

- Place chicken slices on serving platter.

- Beat cream cheese, salsa and mayonnaise in bowl.

- Place heaping tablespoon on top of chicken slices. Serve cold. Serves 4.

Spicy Chicken and Rice

3 cups cooked, sliced chicken
2 cups cooked brown rice
1 (10 ounce) can fiesta nacho cheese soup
1 (10 ounce) can diced tomatoes and green chilies

- Preheat oven to 350°.

- Combine chicken, rice, cheese soup, and tomatoes and green chilies in bowl and mix well.

- Spoon mixture into sprayed 3-quart baking dish. Cover and bake for 45 minutes. Serves 6.

There are more chickens than people in the world.

Chicken-Broccoli Skillet

3 cups cooked, cubed chicken
1 (16 ounce) package frozen broccoli florets
1 (8 ounce) package cubed Velveeta® cheese
⅔ cup mayonnaise

- Combine chicken, broccoli, cheese and ¼ cup water in skillet.

- Cover and cook over medium heat until broccoli is tender-crisp and cheese melts.

- Stir in mayonnaise and heat through, but do not boil. Serves 4.

TIP: Serve over rice.

Best Ever Meatloaf

2 pounds ground turkey
1 (6 ounce) package stuffing mix for chicken
2 eggs, beaten
½ cup ketchup, divided

- Preheat oven to 350°.

- Combine ground turkey, stuffing mix, eggs and ¼ cup ketchup in bowl and mix well.

- Shape meat into oval loaf and palce in center of 9 x 13-inch baking dish.

- Spread remaining ¼ cup ketchup on top of loaf.

- Bake for 1 hour. Serves 8.

Southwestern Steak

1 pound tenderized round steak
Flour
1 (15 ounce) can Mexican stewed tomatoes
2 teaspoons beef bouillon granules

- Preheat oven to 325°.

- Cut beef into serving-size pieces and dredge in flour. Brown steak in sprayed skillet.

- Mix tomatoes and beef bouillon in bowl and pour over steak.

- Cover and bake for 1 hour. Serves 6.

TIP: Put a little olive oil in skillet to brown steak.

Baked Onion-Mushroom Steak

1½ pounds (½ inch thick) round steak
1 (10 ounce) can cream of mushroom soup
1 (1 ounce) packet onion soup mix

- Preheat oven to 325°.

- Place steak in sprayed 9 x 13-inch baking dish.

- Combine mushroom soup and ½ cup water in bowl and pour over steak and sprinkle with onion soup mix.

- Cover and bake for 2 hours. Serves 8.

Red Wine Round Steak

2 pounds (¾ inch thick) round steak
1 (1 ounce) packet onion soup mix
1 cup dry red wine
1 (4 ounce) can sliced mushrooms

- Preheat oven to 325°.

- Remove all fat from steak and cut in serving-size pieces. Brown meat on both sides in sprayed skillet. Place in sprayed 9 x 13-inch baking dish.

- Combine onion soup mix, wine, 1 cup hot water and mushrooms in skillet. Pour over browned steak.

- Cover and bake for 1 hour 20 minutes or until steak is tender. Serves 8 to 10.

Round Steak Sizzle

2 pounds (½ inch thick) round steak
Olive oil
1 onion, thinly sliced
2 (10 ounce) cans tomato bisque soup

- Cut steak into serving-size pieces. Brown meat in a little oil in skillet.

- Mix onion and soup with 1 soup can water in bowl and add to steak. Bring to a boil.

- Turn heat down, cover and simmer for 1 hour 20 minutes. Serves 8.

TIP: *If you want a little breading on the meat, dust meat with flour and a little salt and pepper before browning in skillet.*

Steak-Bake Italiano

2 pounds lean round steak
2 teaspoons Italian seasoning
1 teaspoon garlic salt
2 (15 ounce) cans Italian stewed tomatoes

- Preheat oven to 325°.

- Cut steak into serving-size pieces and brown in sprayed skillet. Place in sprayed 9 x 13-inch baking dish.

- Combine Italian seasoning, garlic salt and stewed tomatoes in bowl. Pour over steak pieces.

- Cover and bake for 1 hour. Serves 8 to 10.

Roasted Garlic Steak

2 (15 ounce) cans tomatoes with roasted garlic and herb
½ cup Italian salad dressing
1½ pounds (¾ inch thick) boneless beef sirloin steak

- Combine tomatoes, dressing and ⅓ cup water in saucepan.

- Broil steaks to desired doneness. Allow 15 minutes for medium. Turn once and brush often with sauce.

- Heat remaining sauce to serve with steak. Serves 6.

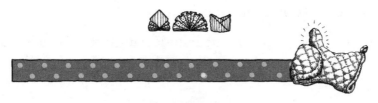

Some mistakes are too much fun to only make once.

Smothered Steak Break

1 large round steak
1 (10 ounce) can golden mushroom soup
1 (1 ounce) packet onion soup mix
⅔ cup milk

- Preheat oven to 325°.

- Cut steak into serving-size pieces and place in sprayed
  9 x 13-inch baking pan.

- Mix soup, dry onion soup and milk in saucepan. Heat just
  enough to mix well. Pour over steak.

- Seal with foil. Bake for 1 hour. Serves 6.

Lickety-Split Peppered Steak

1 (1¼ pound) sirloin steak, cut into strips
1 (16 ounce) package frozen chopped bell peppers and
    onions, thawed
1 (16 ounce) package cubed Mexican Velveeta® cheese
Rice, cooked

- Cook steak strips in sprayed, large skillet for about 10 minutes
  or until no longer pink. Remove steak from skillet and set aside.

- Stir in vegetables and ½ cup water. Simmer vegetables for about
  5 minutes until all liquid cooks out.

- Add cheese. Turn heat to medium-low until cheese melts. Stir
  in steak and serve over rice. Serves 8.

Beef-Broccoli Stack

1 pound beef sirloin steak
1 onion, chopped
1 (10 ounce) can cream of broccoli soup
1 (10 ounce) package frozen chopped broccoli, thawed

- Slice beef across grain into very thin strips. Brown steak strips and onion in large sprayed skillet and stir several times.

- Add a little water, reduce heat and simmer for 10 minutes. Mix in soup and broccoli and heat. Serves 4.

TIP: *Try this over noodles. It's great. The flavors mix really well and the noodles soak it all up.*

Smothered Beef Steak

2 pounds lean round steak
1 cup rice
1 (14 ounce) can beef broth
1 green bell pepper, seeded, chopped

- Cut steak into serving-size pieces and brown in very large skillet.

- Add rice, beef broth, bell peppers and 1 cup water to skillet. Bring to a boil. Reduce heat, cover and simmer for 1 hour. Serves 8.

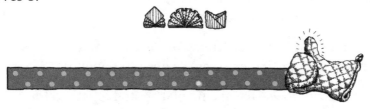

Dry onion soup sprinkled over a roast which will be sealed in foil will make a delicious gravy while the roast is cooking.

Creamy Mushroom Beef

2 (10 ounce) cans golden mushroom soup
½ cup cooking sherry
1 (1 ounce) packet onion soup mix
2 pounds lean beef, cubed

- Preheat oven to 325°.

- Mix soup, sherry and onion soup mix with ¾ cup water in bowl.

- Add steak cubes to sprayed 3-quart baking dish and pour soup mixture on top.

- Bake for about 2 hours. Serves 8 to 10.

TIP: *The creamy gravy with this beef is excellent over noodles, rice or toasted bread.*

Savory Rib Roast

1 tablespoon dried thyme
1 tablespoon dried, crushed rosemary
1 teaspoon rubbed sage
1 (4 - 5 pound) boneless beef roast

- Preheat oven to 350°.

- Combine thyme, rosemary and sage in small bowl and rub over roast. Place roast, fat-side up.

- Bake on rack in large roasting pan for 2 hours to 2 hours 30 minutes or until meat reaches desired doneness.

- Remove roast to warm serving platter and let stand for 10 minutes before slicing. Serves 8 to 10.

Easy Roast Dinner

1 (10 ounce) can cream of mushroom soup
1 (1 ounce) packet onion soup mix
½ cup white wine
1 (4 pound) rump roast

• Preheat oven to 325°.

• Combine mushroom soup, onion soup mix, white wine and
⅓ cup water in bowl.

• Place roast in sprayed roasting pan. Pour soup mixture over
roast.

• Cover and bake for 3 hours 30 minutes to 4 hours. Serves 8.

Tender Beef Roast

1 (3 - 4) pound rump roast
1 (10 ounce) can French onion soup
1 (14 ounce) can beef bouillon
1 teaspoon garlic powder

• Preheat oven to 325°.

• Place roast in sprayed roasting pan. Pour soup and bouillon over
roast and sprinkle with garlic powder.

• Place lid on roasting pan and bake for 3 hours 30 minutes. Pour
pan gravy over roast after it's sliced. Serves 8.

A grudge is a heavy load to carry.
Anonymous

Simple Chuck Roast Meal

1 (3 - 4 pound) boneless rump roast or chuck roast
4 medium potatoes, peeled, cut into pieces
2 onions, quartered
1 (10 ounce) can golden mushroom soup

- Preheat oven to 350°.

- Place seasoned* meat in roasting pan with 1 cup water. Cover and bake for about 1 hour.

- Uncover, add potatoes and onions and continue cooking for additional 1 hour.

- Combine soup and ½ cup water in saucepan. Heat just enough to pour over roast and vegetables.

- Place roaster back in oven just until soup is hot. Serves 8.

TIP: *Everyone seasons food according to their tastes. Salt and pepper work great for this roast. Lemon pepper, garlic salt or seasoned salt are excellent. Season with whatever you have.*

Easy Breezy Brisket

1 (4 - 5 pound) brisket
1 (1 ounce) packet onion soup mix
2 tablespoons Worcestershire sauce
1 cup red wine

- Preheat oven to 325°.

- Place brisket in shallow baking pan. Sprinkle onion soup mix over brisket.

- Pour Worcestershire sauce and red wine in baking pan. Cover and bake for 5 to 6 hours. Serves 8.

Tomorrow Beef Brisket

1 (5 - 6 pound) trimmed beef brisket
1 (1 ounce) packet onion soup mix
1 (10 ounce) bottle steak sauce
1 (12 ounce) bottle barbecue sauce

- Preheat oven to 325°.

- Place brisket, cut-side up in roasting pan.

- Combine onion soup mix, steak sauce and barbecue sauce in bowl and mix. Pour over brisket.

- Cover and cook for 4 to 5 hours or until tender. Remove brisket from pan and pour off drippings. Refrigerate both, separately, overnight.

- The next day, trim all fat from meat, slice and reheat. Skim fat off drippings. Reheat drippings and serve over brisket. Serves 10.

Slow Cookin' Brisket

½ cup liquid hickory-flavored smoke
1 (4 - 5 pound) beef brisket
1 (5 ounce) bottle Worcestershire sauce
¾ cup barbecue sauce

- Pour liquid smoke over brisket. Cover and refrigerate overnight.

- When ready to bake, preheat oven to 275°.

- Drain and pour Worcestershire sauce over brisket. Cover and bake for 6 to 7 hours.

- Uncover and pour barbecue sauce over brisket and bake for additional 30 minutes. Slice very thin across grain. Serves 8.

Taste-of-the-Irish Corned Beef

1 (4 - 5) pound corned beef brisket
4 large potatoes, peeled, quartered
6 carrots, peeled, halved
1 head cabbage

- Place corned beef in roasting pan, cover with water and bring to a boil. Turn heat down and simmer for 3 hours. Add water if necessary.

- Add potatoes and carrots. Cut cabbage into eighths and lay over top of other vegetables.

- Bring to a boil, turn heat down and cook for additional 30 to 40 minutes or until vegetables are done. When slightly cool, slice corned beef across grain. Serves 8.

Corned Beef Suite

1 (5 pound) corned beef brisket
Whole cloves
½ cup maple syrup
Pepper

- Place corned beef in roasting pan with water to cover beef. Bring to a boil. Lower heat and simmer until done. (Allow 30 minutes per pound.)

- When corned beef is cooked, place on rack in shallow pan. Stick whole cloves in crosswise design.

- Preheat oven to 375°.

- Pour syrup over meat and sprinkle with a little pepper.

- Place in oven to brown and glaze for about 15 minutes. When ready to serve, slice beef across grain. Serve hot or at room temperature. Serves 10.

Smothered Beef Patties

1½ pounds ground beef
½ cup chili sauce
½ cup buttery cracker crumbs
1 (14 ounce) can beef broth

- Combine beef, chili sauce and cracker crumbs in bowl and form into 5 or 6 patties.

- Brown patties in sprayed skillet and pour broth over patties.

- Bring to a boil. Reduce heat, cover and simmer for about 40 minutes. Serves 6.

Easy Casserole Supper

1 pound lean ground beef
¼ cup white rice
1 (10 ounce) can French onion soup
1 (3 ounce) can french-fried onions

- Preheat oven to 325°.

- Brown ground beef in sprayed skillet, drain and place in sprayed 7 x 11-inch baking dish.

- Combine rice, onion soup and ½ cup water and add to beef. Cover and bake for 40 minutes.

- Sprinkle fried onions over top and bake uncovered for additional 10 minutes. Serves 4.

Bueno Taco Casserole

2 pounds lean ground beef
1½ cups taco sauce
2 (15 ounce) cans Spanish rice
1 (8 ounce) package shredded Mexican 4-cheese blend, divided

- Preheat oven to 350°.

- Brown ground beef in skillet and drain. Add taco sauce, Spanish rice and half cheese. Spoon into sprayed 3-quart baking dish.

- Cover and bake for 35 minutes. Uncover and sprinkle remaining cheese on top and return to oven for 5 minutes. Serves 8.

Seasoned Onion-Beef Bake

3 pounds lean ground beef
1 (1 ounce) packet onion soup mix
Canola oil
2 (10 ounce) cans French onion soup

- Preheat oven to 350°.

- Combine beef, soup mix and ½ cup water in bowl. Stir well and shape into patties about ½-inch thick.

- Cook in large skillet with a little canola oil and brown on both sides.

- Move patties to sprayed 9 x 13-inch baking dish. Pour soup over patties.

- Cover and bake for about 35 minutes. Serves 8 to 10.

Potato-Beef Bake

1 pound ground beef
1 (10 ounce) can sloppy Joe sauce
1 (10 ounce) can fiesta nacho cheese soup
1 (32 ounce) package frozen hash-brown potatoes, thawed

- Preheat oven to 400°.

- Cook beef in skillet over medium heat until no longer pink and drain.

- Add sloppy Joe sauce and fiesta nacho cheese soup.

- Place hash browns in sprayed 9 x 13-inch baking dish. Top with beef mixture.

- Cover and bake for 25 minutes. Uncover and bake for additional 10 minutes. Serves 6.

TIP: *If you really like a cheesy dish, sprinkle shredded cheddar cheese on top just before serving.*

Tasty Meatloaf Supper

1 (6 ounce) package stuffing mix
1 egg
½ cup salsa
1½ pounds lean ground beef

- Preheat oven to 350°.

- Combine stuffing mix, egg, salsa and ⅓ cup water in bowl and mix well.

- Add ground beef to stuffing mixture.

- Spoon into sprayed 9 x 5-inch loaf pan and bake for 1 hour. Serves 4 to 6.

Savory Herb Meatloaf

1 pound ground round beef
2 (10 ounce) cans cream of mushroom soup
1 (1 ounce) packet dry onion soup mix
1 cup cooked rice

- Preheat oven to 350°.

- Mix all ingredients in bowl. Place into sprayed 9 x 13-inch baking dish and form loaf.

- Bake for 50 minutes. Serves 8.

Rosa's Mexican Beef Bash

1 (13 ounce) bag tortilla chips, divided
2 pounds lean ground beef
1 (15 ounce) can Mexican stewed tomatoes
1 (8 ounce) package shredded Mexican 4-cheese blend

- Preheat oven to 350°.

- Partially crush half bag of chips and place in sprayed 9 x 13-inch baking dish.

- Brown ground beef in sprayed skillet and drain. Add stewed tomatoes and cheese and mix well. Pour beef mixture over crushed chips.

- Finely crush remaining chips and sprinkle over casserole. Bake for 40 minutes. Serves 8.

Beef Patties in Creamy Onion Sauce

1½ pounds lean ground beef
⅓ cup salsa
⅓ cup butter cracker crumbs
1 (10 ounce) can cream of onion soup

- Combine beef, salsa and cracker crumbs in bowl and form into 5 to 6 patties.

- Brown in skillet and reduce heat. Add ¼ cup water and simmer for 15 minutes.

- Combine onion soup and ½ cup water in saucepan, heat and mix. Pour over beef patties. Serves 6.

TIP: *Any time there is a flavorful gravy like this, you have the option to add noodles, rice or bread to soak it up.*

Yummy Creamy Pasta Shells

1¼ pounds lean ground beef
1 onion, chopped
1 (10 ounce) can cream of celery soup
1 (10 ounce) box shells and cheese sauce

- Brown beef and onion in skillet and stir until beef crumbles and is no longer pink. Add soup and mix.

- Prepare shells and cheese according to package directions. Stir into beef mixture.

- Simmer for 20 minutes. Serve hot. Serves 8.

Cheesy Beefy Gnocchi

1 pound lean ground beef
1 (10 ounce) can cheddar cheese soup
1 (10 ounce) can tomato bisque soup
2 cups gnocchi or shell pasta

- Cook beef in skillet until brown and drain.

- Add soups, 1½ cups water and pasta in saucepan. Bring mixture to a boil.

- Cover and cook over medium heat for 12 to 14 minutes or until pasta is done; stir often. Serves 4 to 6.

Meat and Potato Stew

2 pounds beef stew meat
2 (15 ounce) cans new potatoes, drained
1 (15 ounce) can sliced carrots, drained
1 (10 ounce) can French onion soup

- Cook stew meat with about 2 cups water in large pot for 1 hour over medium heat.

- Add potatoes, carrots and onion soup and mix. Bring to a boil, reduce heat and simmer for 30 minutes or until potatoes are tender. Serves 6 to 8.

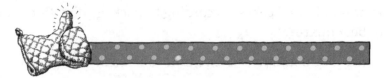

Fat greatly contributes to the flavor of ground beef. The lower the fat content, the drier it will be once cooked.

Stroganoff Stew

2 pounds stew meat
1 (1 ounce) packet onion soup mix
2 (10 ounce) cans golden mushroom soup
1 (8 ounce) carton sour cream

- Preheat oven to 275°.

- Brown stew meat in roasting pan.

- Combine soup mix, soup and 2 cans water in bowl. Pour over stew meat.

- Cover and bake for 6 to 8 hours. When ready to serve, stir in sour cream. Return mixture to oven until thoroughly hot. Serves 6 to 8.

TIP: *Try this over noodles or rice.*

TIP: *This is also great in a slow cooker. It cooks while you are at work or overnight while you sleep.*

Texas Chili Pie

2 (20 ounce) cans chili without beans
1 (16 ounce) package small corn chips
1 onion, chopped
1 (12 ounce) package shredded cheddar cheese

- Preheat oven to 325°.

- Heat chili in saucepan.

- Layer half corn chips, half chili, half onion and half cheese in sprayed 9 x 13-inch baking dish. Repeat layers.

- Bake for 20 minutes or until cheese bubbles. Serves 6.

Cheese 'n Wiener Crescents

8 large wieners
4 slices American cheese, cut into 6 strips each
1 (8 ounce) can refrigerated crescent dinner rolls

- Preheat oven to 375°.

- Slit wieners to within ½-inch of bottom and insert 3 strips cheese in each slit.

- Separate crescent dough into 8 triangles and wrap dough over wiener keeping cheese side up. Place on baking sheet.

- Bake for 12 to 15 minutes or until golden brown. Serves 8.

Chihuahua Dogs

1 (10 ounce) can chili hot dog sauce
1 (10 count) package frankfurters
10 pre-formed taco shells
Shredded cheddar cheese

- Place hot dog sauce in saucepan and heat.

- Place frank in each taco shell. Top with heated chili sauce and cheese; place in microwave-safe dish.

- Place in microwave and heat for 30 seconds or until frankfurters are warm. Serves 5 to 7.

Plum Peachy Pork Roast

1 (4 - 5 pound) boneless pork loin roast
1 (12 ounce) jar plum jelly
½ cup peach preserves
½ teaspoon ginger

- Preheat oven to 325°.

- Place roast in shallow baking pan and bake for 1 hour.

- Turn roast to brown and bake for additional 1 hour.

- Heat jelly, peach preserves and ginger in saucepan. Brush roast generously with preserve mixture after it is done.

- Bake for an additional 15 minutes and baste again.

- Serve preserve mixture and liquid in baking pan with roast. Serves 6.

Hawaiian Pork Tenderloin

1 (2 pound) lean pork tenderloin, cut in 1-inch cubes
1 (15 ounce) can pineapple chunks with liquid
1 (12 ounce) bottle chili sauce
1 teaspoon ground ginger

- Place all ingredients in skillet.

- Cover and simmer for 1 hour 30 minutes. Serves 8.

A smile is the best thing you can wear.
Grandma Mullins

Hearty Pork Tenderloin

3 pounds pork tenderloin, cut into strips
1 (15 ounce) can stewed tomatoes
1 (1 ounce) packet savory herb with garlic soup mix
2 tablespoons Worcestershire sauce

- Preheat oven to 325°.

- Place tenderloin strips in sprayed roasting pan.

- Mix remaining ingredients in bowl and spread over meat.

- Cover and bake for 1 hour 20 minutes. Serves 6.

Tenderloin with Apricot Sauce

3 pounds pork tenderloin
1 cup apricot preserves
⅓ cup lemon juice
⅓ cup ketchup

- Preheat oven to 325°.

- Place tenderloin in sprayed roasting pan. Combine preserves, lemon juice and ketchup in bowl and pour over pork.

- Cover and bake for 1 hour 20 minutes. Baste once during cooking. Serves 6.

TIP: *This tenderloin is great with the apricot sauce. If you want to serve a heartier dish, add rice and serve tenderloin on top.*

Piggy Pork Picante

1 pound pork tenderloin, cubed
1 (1 ounce) packet taco seasoning
1 cup chunky salsa
⅓ cup peach preserves

- Toss pork with taco seasoning and brown in skillet.

- Stir in salsa and preserves. Bring to a boil.

- Lower heat and simmer for 30 minutes. Serves 4.

Apple-Topped Tenderloin

1½ cups hickory marinade, divided
1 (3 - 4 pound) pork tenderloin
1 (20 ounce) can apple pie filling
¾ teaspoon ground cinnamon

- Combine 1 cup marinade and tenderloin in resealable plastic bag. Marinate in refrigerator for at least 1 hour.

- When ready to cook, preheat oven to 325°.

- Remove tenderloin and discard used marinade.

- Cook tenderloin for 1 hour and baste twice with ¼ cup marinade. Let stand for 10 or 15 minutes before slicing.

- Combine pie filling, remaining ¼ cup marinade and cinnamon in saucepan and heat. Serve sauce over sliced tenderloin. Serves 8.

Honey-Ham Slice

⅓ cup orange juice
⅓ cup honey
1 teaspoon mustard
1 (1 inch thick) slice fully cooked ham

- Combine orange juice, honey and mustard in saucepan, cook slowly for 10 minutes and stir occasionally.

- Brush ham with orange glaze. Place in broiling pan about 3 inches from heat.

- Broil for 8 minutes on first side. Turn ham slice over. Brush with glaze again and broil for additional 6 to 8 minutes. Serves 4.

Cran-Apple Ham

1 cup apple juice, divided
1 tablespoon cornstarch
1 cup whole cranberry sauce
1 center-cut ham slice or 1 (2 - 3 pound) smoked, boneless ham

- Preheat oven to 350°.

- Combine ¼-cup apple juice and cornstarch in medium saucepan over low heat and stir constantly until cornstarch is smooth.

- Add remaining apple juice. Bring to a boil and cook on medium heat, stirring constantly, until mixture thickens.

- Stir in cranberry sauce and heat for 2 to 3 minutes.

- Place ham slice in shallow baking pan. Spread sauce over ham slice, bake for 20 to 30 minutes and baste ham with sauce 2 to 3 times.

- Serve warmed sauce with ham. (If you use boneless ham, cook 45 to 60 minutes longer.) Serves 4.

Ham and Sweet Potato Reward

3 tablespoons dijon-style mustard, divided
1 (3 - 4 pound) boneless smoked ham
½ cup honey or packed brown sugar
1 (29 ounce) can sweet potatoes

- Preheat oven at 325°.

- Spread 2 tablespoons mustard on ham. Place ham in sprayed shallow baking pan and bake for 20 minutes.

- Combine remaining mustard with honey or brown sugar in bowl and spread over ham.

- Add sweet potatoes, baste with sauce and bake for 20 minutes. Serves 6 to 8.

Tempting Mustard Ham

1 (1 inch thick) slice cooked ham
2 teaspoons dry mustard
⅓ cup honey
⅓ cup cooking wine

- Preheat oven to 350°.

- Rub ham slice with 1 teaspoon mustard on each side. Place in shallow baking pan.

- Combine honey and wine in bowl and pour over ham. Bake for about 35 minutes. Serves 4.

Speedy Ham and Veggies

1 (16 ounce) package frozen mixed vegetables
1 (10 ounce) can cream of celery soup
2 cups cooked, cubed ham
½ teaspoon dried basil

- Cook vegetables according to package directions. Add soup, ham and basil.

- Cook until thoroughly hot and serve immediately. Serves 4 to 6.

Peach-Pineapple Baked Ham

4 tablespoons dijon-style mustard, divided
1 (3 - 4) pound boneless smoked ham
1 cup peach preserves
1 cup pineapple preserves

- Preheat oven to 325°.

- Spread 2 tablespoons mustard on ham. Place ham in sprayed shallow baking pan and bake for 20 minutes.

- Combine remaining 2 tablespoons mustard and preserves and heat in microwave oven for 20 seconds. (If you cook on stove, place sauce in small saucepan on low heat for 2 to 3 minutes.)

- Pour over ham and bake for additional 15 minutes. Serves 8 to 10.

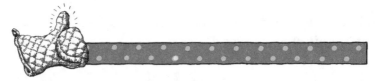

When frying ham steaks or slices, cut slits in the fat around the edges and the ham will not curl up around the edges.

"Giddy-Up" Pork Chops

6 boneless pork chops
½ cup salsa
½ cup honey or packed brown sugar
1 teaspoon soy sauce

- Preheat oven to 325°.

- Brown pork chops in sprayed ovenproof pan.

- Combine salsa, honey or brown sugar and soy sauce
  in microwave-safe bowl and heat for 20 to 30 seconds
  in microwave.

- Pour salsa mixture over pork chops; cover and bake for about
  45 minutes or until pork chops are tender. Serves 6.

TIP: *You can add an interesting "giddy-up" with ¼ teaspoon crushed
red pepper flakes. It's not necessary, however, for a delicious dish.*

Pork Chops in Cream Gravy

4 (¼ inch thick) pork chops
Flour
Olive oil
2¼ cups milk

- Dip pork chops in flour. Brown chops on both sides in a little oil
  in skillet. Remove chops from skillet.

- Add about 2 tablespoons flour to skillet, brown lightly while
  stirring constantly.

- Slowly stir in milk to make gravy. Return chops to skillet
  with gravy.

- Cover and simmer on low burner for about 40 minutes. Serves 4.

TIP: *Here's another great recipe to serve over noodles or rice.*

Picky Pork-Potato Chop

6 boneless or loin pork chops
1 (14 ounce) can chicken broth
2 (1 ounce) packets onion soup mix
6 new (red) potatoes, sliced

- Brown pork chops in large sprayed skillet.

- Combine chicken broth and soup mix.

- Place potatoes with pork chops and pour soup mixture over pork chops and potatoes.

- Heat to boiling, reduce heat; cover and simmer for about 45 minutes or until pork chops and potatoes are fork-tender. Serves 6.

Cranberry Pork Chops

6 - 8 thick pork chops
Flour
2 cups fresh or frozen cranberries
1 cup sugar

- Preheat oven to 350°.

- Coat pork chops in flour and brown in sprayed skillet. Place in shallow baking dish.

- Add cranberries, sugar and ½ cup water. Cover and bake for 30 minutes. Uncover and continue baking for additional 30 minutes. Serves 6 to 8.

TIP: *If spraying the skillet isn't enough to brown the chops the way you like, pour in a little oil.*

Mexicali Pork Chops

1 (1 ounce) packet taco seasoning
4 (½ inch thick) boneless pork chops
1 tablespoon olive oil
Salsa

- Rub taco seasoning over pork chops. Brown pork chops in oil in skillet over medium heat.

- Add 2 tablespoons water, turn heat to low and simmer pork chops for about 40 minutes. Check to see if a little more water is needed.

- Spoon salsa over pork chops to serve. Serves 4.

Apple Pork Chops

4 butterflied pork chops
2 apples, peeled, cored
2 teaspoons butter
2 tablespoons brown sugar

- Preheat oven to 350°.

- Place pork chops in sprayed shallow baking dish.

- Cover and bake for 30 minutes. Uncover and place apple halves on top of pork chops. Add a little butter and a little brown sugar on each apple.

- Bake for additional 15 minutes. Serves 4.

TIP: *Seasoning is always up to you, but salt and pepper are plenty for these pork chops.*

Lemon-Baked Pork Chops

¾ cup ketchup
¾ cup packed brown sugar
¼ cup lemon juice
4 butterflied pork chops

- Preheat oven to 325°.

- Combine ketchup, ½ cup water, brown sugar and lemon juice in bowl.

- Place pork chops in sprayed 7 x 11-inch baking dish and pour sauce over pork chops.

- Cover and bake for 50 minutes. Serves 4.

Spicy Pork Chops

4 - 6 pork chops
1 large onion
1 bell pepper, seeded
1 (10 ounce) can diced tomatoes and green chilies

- Preheat oven to 350°.

- Brown pork chops in sprayed skillet. Place chops in sprayed baking dish.

- Cut onion and bell pepper into large chunks and place on chops. Pour tomatoes and green chilies over chops.

- Cover and bake for 45 minutes. Serves 4 to 6.

Sassy Saucy Pork Chops

4 (½ inch thick) pork chops
1 tablespoon olive oil
1 (10 ounce) can cream of onion soup
2 tablespoons soy sauce

- Brown pork chops in oil in skillet, cook chops for about 15 minutes and drain.

- Remove pork chops and set aside. Add soup and soy sauce to skillet. Heat to boil and reduce heat.

- Return chops to pan, cover and simmer for about 20 minutes. Serves 4.

Sunny Orange Pork Chops

6 - 8 medium thick pork chops
¼ cup (½ stick) butter
2¼ cups orange juice
⅓ cup orange marmalade

- Brown both sides of pork chops in butter in hot skillet.

- Pour orange juice over chops. Cover and simmer until done, about 1 hour. (Time will vary with thickness of pork chops.)

- Add more orange juice, if necessary. During last few minutes of cooking, add orange marmalade. Serves 6 to 8.

TIP: *This makes delicious gravy to serve over rice.*

Tangy Pork Chops

4 - 6 pork chops
¼ cup Worcestershire sauce
¼ cup ketchup
½ cup honey

- Preheat oven to 325°.

- Brown pork chops in skillet. Place in shallow baking dish.

- Combine Worcestershire sauce, ketchup and honey in bowl.
  Pour over pork chops.

- Cover and bake for 45 minutes. Serves 4 to 6.

Sweet and Savory Pork Chops

4 - 6 (1 inch thick) boneless pork chops, trimmed
½ cup grape, apple or plum jelly
½ cup chili sauce or hot ketchup
Soy sauce or teriyaki sauce

- Preheat oven to 325°.

- Brown pork chops in skillet. Transfer browned pork chops to
  shallow baking dish.

- Combine jelly and chili sauce or ketchup in bowl and spread over
  pork chops.

- Bake for 15 minutes, baste with sauce and Bake for additional 15
  minutes or until pork chops are tender. Serve with soy sauce or
  teriyaki sauce. Serves 4 to 6.

Sweet-and-Sour Spareribs

4 pounds pork spareribs
1 (6 ounce) can frozen lemonade concentrate, thawed
½ teaspoon garlic salt
⅓ cup soy sauce

- Preheat oven to 350°.

- Place spareribs, meaty-side down in shallow, sprayed roasting pan with a little water. Cover and cook for 40 minutes.

- Remove cover, drain fat and return ribs to oven. Bake for additional 30 minutes. Drain fat again.

- Combine remaining ingredients in bowl and brush on ribs.

- Reduce temperature to 325°. Cover and bake for 1 hour or until tender and brush occasionally with sauce. Serves 4 to 6.

Spunky Spareribs

5 - 6 pounds spareribs
1 (6 ounce) can frozen orange juice concentrate, thawed
2 teaspoons Worcestershire sauce
½ teaspoon garlic powder

- Preheat oven to 350°.

- Place spareribs in sprayed shallow baking pan, meat-side down.

- Roast for 30 minutes. Turn ribs and roast for additional 30 minutes. Drain off fat.

- Combine remaining ingredients in bowl and brush mixture on ribs.

- Reduce heat to 300°. Cover and roast for 2 hours or until tender, basting occasionally. Serves 6 to 8.

Orange-Sauced Spareribs

4 - 5 pounds pork spareribs
1 (6 ounce) can frozen orange juice concentrate, thawed
½ teaspoon garlic salt
⅔ cup honey

- Preheat oven to 350°.

- Place ribs, meaty-side down in shallow roasting pan. Bake for 30 minutes.

- Drain off fat and turn ribs. Bake for additional 30 minutes.

- Combine remaining ingredients in bowl and brush on ribs. Reduce temperature to 325°.

- Cover and bake for 1 hour 30 minutes or until tender; brush with sauce several times. Serves 4 to 6.

Barbecued Spareribs

3 - 4 pounds pork spareribs or country-style pork ribs, trimmed
1 cup hot ketchup or chili sauce
½ cup honey or packed brown sugar
1 teaspoon liquid smoke

- Preheat oven to 350°.

- Place spareribs on sprayed broiler pan and bake for 1 hour 30 minutes

- Combine ketchup, honey or brown sugar and liquid smoke in small saucepan and simmer for 2 to 3 minutes.

- Baste spareribs generously on both sides with ketchup mixture.

- Reduce heat to 300°. Bake for additional 1 hour 30 minutes or until tender; baste generously every 15 to 20 minutes. Serves 4.

German-Style Ribs and Kraut

3 - 4 pounds baby-back pork ribs or country-style pork ribs,
   trimmed
3 potatoes, peeled, sliced
1 (32 ounce) jar refrigerated sauerkraut, drained
¼ cup pine nuts, toasted

- Brown ribs in sprayed, large heavy pan on all sides. Add 1 cup water.

- Bring to a boil, turn down heat and simmer for about 2 hours or until ribs are very tender.

- Add potatoes and cook on low heat for 20 minutes. Add sauerkraut and continue cooking until potatoes are done.

- Sprinkle pine nuts on ribs and sauerkraut immediately before serving. Serves 4.

Tequila Baby Back Ribs

4 pounds baby back pork ribs
1 (12 ounce) bottle tequila-lime marinade, divided

- Cut ribs in lengths to fit in large, resealable plastic bag.

- Place ribs in bag, add ¾ cup marinade, seal bag and shake to coat.

- Marinate in refrigerator overnight. Place ribs in sprayed shallow baking dish and discard used marinade.

- When ready to bake, preheat oven to 375°.

- Cover ribs with foil and bake for 30 minutes. Remove from oven and spread a little extra marinade over ribs.

- Lower heat to 300° and cook for 1 hour. Uncover to let ribs brown and bake for additional 30 minutes. Serves 3 to 4.

Italian Sausage and Ravioli

1 pound sweet Italian pork sausage, casing removed
1 (26 ounce) jar extra chunky mushroom and green pepper
    spaghetti sauce
1 (24 ounce) package frozen cheese-filled ravioli, cooked, drained
Grated parmesan cheese

- Cook sausage according to package directions in roasting pan
  over medium heat or until brown and no longer pink; stir to
  separate meat.

- Stir in spaghetti sauce. Heat to boiling. Add ravioli, heat
  through and stir occasionally.

- Pour into serving dish and sprinkle with parmesan cheese.
  Serves 8.

Cranberry Sauce Extra

1 (14 ounce) carton strawberry glaze
1 (12 ounce) package frozen cranberries
½ cup orange juice
¼ cup sugar

- Combine glaze, cranberries, orange juice and sugar in saucepan.
  Heat to a boil and stir constantly.

- Reduce heat, simmer for 10 minutes or until cranberries pop
  and stir often.

- Refrigerate for several hours before serving. Serve with pork or
  ham. Yields 1½ pints.

Crispy Flounder

⅓ cup mayonnaise
1 pound flounder fillets
1 cup seasoned breadcrumbs
¼ cup grated parmesan cheese

• Preheat oven to 375°.

• Place mayonnaise in small dish. Coat fish with mayonnaise and dip in breadcrumbs to coat well.

• Arrange in sprayed 9 x 13-inch baking dish and cover with parmesan cheese. Bake for 15 to 20 minutes. Serves 2 to 4.

Fried Haddock Fillets

1½ cups lemon-lime soda
1 pound haddock fillets
2 cups biscuit mix
Olive oil

• Pour soda in shallow bowl, add fillets and marinate for 15 minutes.

• In separate shallow bowl, combine biscuit mix. Remove fish from soda and coat with biscuit mix.

• Heat about ¼-inch oil in large skillet. Fry fish for about 3 minutes on each side or until fish flakes with fork. Drain on paper towels. Serve 6.

Fish and Chips

1 cup mayonnaise
2 tablespoons fresh lime juice
3 - 4 fish fillets, rinsed, dried
1½ cups crushed corn chips

- Preheat oven to 425°.

- Mix mayonnaise and lime juice in bowl. Spread on both sides of fish fillets.

- Place crushed corn chips on wax paper and dredge both sides of fish in crushed chips. Shake off excess chips.

- Place fillets on foil-covered baking sheet and bake for 15 minutes or until fish flakes. Serve with lime wedges. Serves 4.

Red Fish Barbecue

2 pounds red fish fillets
1 (8 ounce) bottle Italian dressing
1 (12 ounce) can beer
Several dashes hot sauce

- Place fish in glass baking dish. Pour Italian dressing, beer and hot sauce over fish.

- Cover and marinate in refrigerator for at least 2 hours.

- When ready to cook, drain fish, discard marinade and place in microwave-safe dish.

- Microwave fish for about 2 to 4 minutes per pound. Serves 4 to 6.

Butter-Baked Fish Fillets

½ cup (1 stick) butter
4 - 6 cod or flounder fillets
Lemon juice

- Preheat oven to 400°.

- Place butter in shallow baking dish in very hot oven until it melts and browns slightly.

- Place fillets in hot butter and cook for 10 minutes. Turn and baste with pan juices. Sprinkle fish with lemon juice.

- Bake for additional few minutes or until fish flakes easily. Serves 4.

Lemon-Baked Fish

1 pound sole or halibut fillets
¼ cup (½ stick) butter, melted, divided
2 teaspoons Italian seasoning, divided
2 tablespoons lemon juice

- Preheat oven to 375°.

- Place fish fillets in sprayed, shallow pan. Sprinkle with 1 teaspoon seasoning and butter.

- Bake for 8 to 10 minutes. Turn and bake for additional 6 minutes or until fish flakes.

- Combine remaining butter with remaining seasoning and lemon juice. Serve over warm fish fillets. Serves 2 to 4.

Orange Roughy with Peppers

1½ pounds orange roughy
Olive oil
2 red bell peppers, seeded, julienned
1 teaspoon dried thyme leaves

- Cut fish into serving-size pieces.

- Heat a little oil in skillet. Layer bell pepper and thyme. Place fish on top.

- Turn burner on high until fish is hot enough to begin cooking.

- Lower heat, cover and cook fish for 15 to 20 minutes or until fish flakes easily. Serves 4.

Baked Halibut Supreme

2 (1 inch thick) halibut steaks
1 (8 ounce) carton sour cream
½ cup grated parmesan cheese
¾ teaspoon dill weed

- Preheat oven to 325°.

- Place halibut in sprayed 9 x 13-inch baking dish.

- Combine sour cream, parmesan cheese and dill weed. Spoon over halibut. Cover and bake at for about 20 minutes.

- Uncover and bake for additional 10 minutes or until fish flakes easily with fork. Serves 6 to 8.

Broiled Salmon Steaks

4 (1 inch thick) salmon steaks
Garlic salt
Worcestershire sauce
¼ - ½ cup butter, melted

- Place salmon steaks on sprayed baking sheet and sprinkle both sides with garlic salt.

- Splash Worcestershire sauce and butter on top of each salmon steak and broil for 2 to 3 minutes.

- Remove from oven and turn each steak. Splash more Worcestershire sauce and butter on top and broil for 2 to 3 more minutes.

- Top with a little melted butter just before serving. Serves 4.

TIP: *It's easy to cook fish too long. Just make sure it is still moist inside, not dry on the outside and flakes as you pull meat apart with fork.*

Scrumptious Salmon Bites

1 (15 ounce) can pink salmon with liquid
1 egg
½ cup cracker crumbs
1 teaspoon baking powder

- Drain salmon and set aside liquid. Remove bones and skin.

- Stir in egg and cracker crumbs with salmon in bowl.

- In separate bowl, combine baking powder to ¼ cup salmon liquid. (Mixture will foam.) After foaming, add to salmon mixture.

- Drop teaspoonfuls of mixture on hot skillet. Brown lightly on both sides. Serve hot. Serves 4 to 6.

Curried Red Snapper

1½ pounds fresh red snapper
1 teaspoon curry powder
¼ cup milk

• Preheat oven to 350°.

• Place snapper in sprayed 9 x 13-inch baking pan.

• Combine curry powder and milk and mix well. Spoon over snapper.

• Bake for 25 minutes or until fish flakes easily with fork. Serves 4.

TIP: *There is a package of frozen chopped bell peppers, onions and celery in the frozen foods section called Seasoning Blend. You can cook 1 cup of it for a few minutes in a little butter in the baking dish, add the snapper on top and follow the recipe above. The snapper is great just as it is, but some people like the hint of vegetables in the sauce. The real tip here is that you don't have to buy vegetables and chop them. Seasoning Blend makes cooking really easy.*

Terrific Tuna Toast

1 (10 ounce) can cream of chicken soup
1 (6 ounce) can tuna in water, drained
2 slices thick Texas (thick) toast
1 tomato, cubed

• Combine soup and tuna in saucepan and stir to break up chunks of tuna.

• Brown Texas toast on both sides. Pour soup mixture over toast.

• Sprinkle tomatoes over soup mixture. Serve immediately. Serves 2.

Cheesy Tuna Bake

1 (8 ounce) package crescent rolls, divided
1 (6 ounce) can solid white tuna in water, drained, flaked
1 (15 ounce) can cut asparagus, drained
1 cup shredded cheddar cheese

- Preheat oven to 375°.

- Form 7-inch square using 4 crescent rolls. Pinch edges together to seal. Place in sprayed 8-inch square baking pan.

- Layer tuna, asparagus and cheese on top.

- Form remaining 4 crescent rolls into 1 square. Place on top of cheese.

- Bake for about 20 minutes or until top is golden brown and cheese bubbles. Serves 6.

Simple Shrimp Newburg

1 (10 ounce) can cream of shrimp soup
1 teaspoon seafood seasoning
1 (1 pound) package frozen cooked salad shrimp, thawed
White rice, cooked

- Combine soup, ¼ cup water and seafood seasoning in saucepan and bring to a boil.

- Reduce heat and stir in shrimp. Heat thoroughly. Serve over white rice. Serves 4.

Broiled Lemon-Garlic Shrimp

1 pound shrimp, peeled, veined
1 teaspoon garlic salt
2 tablespoons lemon juice
2 tablespoons butter

- Place shrimp in shallow baking pan. Sprinkle with garlic salt and lemon juice and dot with butter.

- Broil on 1 side for 3 minutes. Turn and broil for additional 3 minutes. Serves 4.

TIP: *If shrimp are large, split them down middle and spread them out like a butterfly before seasoning.*

Skillet Shrimp Magic

2 teaspoons olive oil
2 pounds shrimp, peeled, veined
⅔ cup herb-garlic marinade with lemon juice
¼ cup finely chopped green onions with tops

- Heat oil in large non-stick skillet. Add shrimp and marinade.

- Cook, stirring often, until shrimp turn pink. Stir in green onions. Serves 4 to 6.

TIP: *This is a wonderful shrimp dish. Serve as is or over rice or your favorite pasta.*

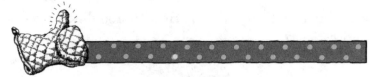

You do not really understand something unless you can explain it to your grandmother. Albert Einstein

Easy Boiled Shrimp

3 pounds fresh shrimp
2 teaspoons seafood seasoning
½ cup vinegar
1 teaspoon salt

• Remove heads from shrimp.

• Place shrimp, salt, seasoning and vinegar in large saucepan.
  Cover shrimp with water and bring to a boil.

• Reduce heat and boil for 10 minutes. Remove from heat, drain
  and refrigerate. Serves 8.

Simple Summer Shrimp Supper

1½ pounds cooked, peeled shrimp
1 small head lettuce, chopped
1 (14 ounce) jar artichokes, quartered, drained
1 avocado, sliced

• Combine all ingredients in bowl. Serve 4.

TIP: *This shrimp supper is great just as it is, but if you want cocktail or
a creamy dressing, just add it. You don't need it, but some people
like shrimp with some kind of dressing.*

*The most important thing to remember
about cooking fish is not to overcook it.
The internal temperature should be about
145° and the flesh should be opaque.
Don't let fish dry out.*

Super Crab-Potato Salad

5 potatoes, peeled, cubed
2 (8 ounce) packages imitation crabmeat, chopped
1 cup finely chopped onion
2 cups mayonnaise

- Place potatoes in saucepan covered with water, bring to a boil and cook for about 20 minutes or until tender. Drain and cool.

- Combine potatoes, crabmeat and onion in large bowl. Toss with mayonnaise.

- Refrigerate for about 3 hours before serving. Serves 4 to 6.

Crusted Baked Oysters

1 cup oysters, drained, rinsed
2 cups cracker crumbs
¼ cup (½ stick) butter, melted
½ cup milk

- Preheat oven to 350°.

- Make alternate layers of oysters, cracker crumbs and butter in sprayed 8-inch square baking dish.

- Warm milk in saucepan and pour over layers. Bake for about 15 to 20 minutes. Serves 4.

*I went to a seafood disco last week...
and pulled a mussel.*

Desserts

Brandied-Apple Dessert

1 (10 ounce) loaf pound cake
1 (20 ounce) can apple pie filling
½ teaspoon ground allspice
2 tablespoons brandy

- Slice pound cake and place on individual dessert plates.

- Combine pie filling, allspice and brandy in saucepan. Heat and stir just until mixture heats thoroughly.

- Place several spoonfuls over cake. Serves 8.

Caramel-Apple Delight

3 (2 ounce) Snickers® candy bars, frozen
2 Granny Smith apples, chopped
1 (12 ounce) carton whipped topping
1 (3 ounce) package instant vanilla pudding

- Smash frozen candy bars in wrappers with hammer.

- Mix all ingredients in bowl and refrigerate. Serves 4 to 6.

TIP: *Place in a pretty crystal bowl or serve in individual sherbet glasses.*

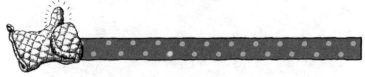

Go easy on yourself. Serving ice cream or sorbet for dessert is a great idea. For a personal touch offer bowls of different toppings and let guests create their own sundae.

Sweet Blueberry Fluff

1 (20 ounce) can blueberry pie filling
1 (20 ounce) can crushed pineapple, drained
1 (14 ounce) can sweetened, condensed milk
1 (8 ounce) carton whipped topping

- Mix pie filling, pineapple and sweetened condensed milk in bowl.

- Fold in whipped topping. Pour into parfait glasses. Refrigerate. Serves 6 to 8.

Lemon Pie Treat

1 (3 ounce) package lemon pie filling mix
⅓ cup sugar
1 egg, slightly beaten
½ (8 ounce) carton whipped topping

- Mix pie filling, sugar and egg with ¼ cup water in saucepan until smooth. Slowly add another 1¾ cups water.

- Cook, stirring constantly, over medium heat until mixture comes to a full boil. Remove from heat and cool to room temperature.

- Fold in whipped topping and spoon into individual dessert dishes. Serves 6.

" A hard thing about business is minding your own." Anonymous

Fluffy Grape Whip

1 cup grape juice
2 cups miniature marshmallows
2 tablespoons lemon juice
1 (8 ounce) carton whipping cream, whipped

- Heat grape juice in saucepan to boiling.

- Add marshmallows and stir constantly until they melt.

- Add lemon juice and cool to room temperature.

- Fold in whipped cream and spoon into individual serving dishes. Refrigerate. Serves 4.

Orange-Apricot Pudding

1 (3.4 ounce) package vanilla pudding (not instant)
1 (15 ounce) can apricot halves with liquid
1 (11 ounce) can mandarin oranges, drained
1 (8 ounce) carton whipped topping

- Cook pudding, stirring constantly with 1¼ cups apricot liquid in saucepan over medium heat. (Add water to apricot liquid to make 1¼ cups if necessary.) Cool.

- Add oranges and cut-up apricots. Refrigerate until mixture begins to thicken.

- Fold in whipped topping. Spoon into 6 individual sherbet dishes. Serves 6.

Chocolate-Vanilla-Almond Parfait

1 (3 ounce) box instant chocolate pudding mix
1 (3 ounce) box instant vanilla pudding mix
4 cups milk, divided
2 cups slivered almonds

• Use 2 different bowls to prepare the 2 pudding mixes. Combine
  each with 2 cups milk according to package directions. Cover
  tightly with plastic wrap and refrigerate.

• Place slivered almonds in dry skillet over medium heat. Stir
  until almonds brown evenly.

• Spoon small amounts of chocolate pudding, then vanilla
  pudding to parfait or stemmed glass.

• Repeat layers and garnish with almonds. Chill before serving.
  Serves 8.

Spiced Amaretto Peaches

4½ cups peeled, sliced fresh peaches
½ cup amaretto liqueur
½ cup sour cream
½ cup packed brown sugar

• Lay peaches in 2-quart baking dish. Pour amaretto over peaches
  and spread with sour cream. Sprinkle brown sugar evenly over all.

• Broil mixture until it heats thoroughly and sugar melts. Serves 6.

• You may make your own amaretto by following the recipe for
  amaretto on page 52. It's great.

Homestead Peach Bake

2 (15 ounce) cans peach halves, drained
1 cup packed brown sugar
1 cup round, buttery cracker crumbs
½ cup (1 stick) butter, melted

- Preheat oven to 325º.

- Layer peaches, brown sugar and cracker crumbs in sprayed
  2-quart baking dish until all ingredients are used.

- Pour melted butter over casserole. Bake for 35 minutes or
  until cracker crumbs are light brown. Serve hot or at room
  temperature. Serves 4.

Divine Strawberries

This is wonderful served over pound cake or just served in sherbet glasses.

1 quart fresh strawberries, cored
1 (20 ounce) can pineapple chunks, well drained
2 bananas, sliced
2 (16 ounce) carton strawberry glaze

- Cut strawberries in half (or in quarters if strawberries are
  very large).

- Combine strawberries, pineapple chunks and bananas in bowl.

- Fold in strawberry glaze and refrigerate. Serves 6 to 8.

Strawberry Trifle

1 (5 ounce) package French vanilla instant pudding mix
1 (10 ounce) loaf pound cake
½ cup sherry
2 cups fresh strawberries, sliced

- Prepare pudding according to package directions.

- Place layer of pound cake slices in bottom of 8-inch crystal bowl.

- Sprinkle with ¼ cup sherry.

- Add layer of strawberries. Layer half pudding. Repeat layers.

- Refrigerate overnight or for several hours. Serves 6 to 8.

Winter Wonderland Dessert

28 chocolate cream-filled chocolate cookies, divided
2¾ cups milk
3 (3.4 ounce) packages instant pistachio pudding
1 (8 ounce) carton whipped topping

- Crush cookies and set aside ⅔ cup. Place crushed cookies in 9 x 13-inch dish.

- Combine milk and pistachio pudding in bowl. Mix for about 2 minutes or until it thickens. Pour over crushed cookies.

- Spread whipped topping over pistachio pudding.

- Sprinkle set aside cookies crumbs over whipped topping and refrigerate overnight before serving. Serves 12.

Divinity Heaven

2 (7 ounce) jars marshmallow creme
3 cups sugar
Pinch of salt
⅔ cup chopped pecans

- Put marshmallow creme in large bowl.

- Combine ½ cup water with sugar and pinch of salt in saucepan. Bring to a rolling boil for exactly 2 minutes.

- Pour sugar mixture into marshmallow cream and stir quickly.

- Add pecans and drop teaspoonfuls of mixture onto wax paper. Serves 8.

Coffee Mallow

3 cups miniature marshmallows
½ cup hot, strong coffee
1 (8 ounce) carton whipping cream, whipped
½ teaspoon vanilla

- Combine marshmallows and coffee in large saucepan. Cook on low heat, stirring constantly until marshmallows melt.

- Cool mixture to room temperature. Fold in whipped cream and vanilla.

- Pour into individual dessert glasses. Refrigerate until ready to serve. Serves 4 to 6.

Easy Boiled Custard

1 (14 ounce) can sweetened condensed milk
1 quart milk
4 eggs
½ teaspoon vanilla

- Combine sweetened condensed milk and milk and heat in double boiler.

- Beat eggs well in bowl. Slowly pour milk, a little at a time, over eggs, stirring constantly.

- Gradually add eggs to milk and cook on low for 5 to 10 minutes, stirring constantly, until mixture thickens.

- Stir in vanilla and refrigerate. Serves 8.

TIP: *This may be served in custard cups or stemmed glasses.*

Smooth Mango Cream

2 soft mangoes
½ gallon vanilla ice cream, softened
1 (6 ounce) can frozen lemonade concentrate, thawed
1 (8 ounce) carton whipped topping

- Peel mangoes, slice around seeds and cut into small chunks.

- Mix ice cream, lemonade and whipped topping in large bowl. Fold in mango chunks.

- Quickly spoon mixture into parfait or sherbet glasses and cover with plastic wrap. Place in freezer. Serves 6 to 8.

Almond-Capped Peach Sundaes

1 (1 pint) carton vanilla ice cream
¾ cup peach preserves, warmed
¼ cup chopped almonds, toasted
¼ cup flaked coconut

- Divide ice cream into 4 sherbet dishes. Top with preserves.

- Sprinkle with almonds and coconut. Serves 4.

Amaretto Ice Cream

1 (8 ounce) carton whipping cream, whipped
1 (1 pint) carton vanilla ice cream, softened
⅓ cup plus ¼ cup amaretto liqueur, divided
⅓ cup chopped almonds, toasted

- Combine whipped cream, ice cream and ⅓ cup amaretto in bowl. Freeze in sherbet glasses.

- When ready to serve, drizzle a little remaining amaretto over top of each individual serving and sprinkle with toasted almonds. Serves 4.

We are all time travelers moving at the speed of exactly 60 seconds per hour.

Chocolate-Coconut Mist

2 (14 ounce) packages flaked coconut
2 tablespoons butter, melted
1⅓ cups semi-sweet chocolate chips, melted
3 quarts mint chocolate chip ice cream

- Toss coconut, butter and chocolate in bowl until mixture blends well.

- Shape ⅓ cupfuls into 2½-inch nests on baking sheet covered with wax paper. Refrigerate until firm.

- Just before serving top each nest with ½ cup ice cream. Serves 10.

Cookies and Cream Dessert

25 Oreo® cookies, crushed
½ gallon vanilla ice cream, softened
1 (15 ounce) can chocolate syrup
1 (12 ounce) carton whipped topping

- Press crushed cookies in 9 x 13-inch baking dish. Spread ice cream over cookies.

- Pour syrup over ice cream and top with whipped topping. Freeze overnight.

- Slice into squares to serve. Serves 10.

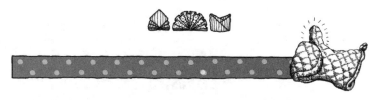

Peanuts have a lot of protein and are good ingredients in high energy drinks.

Fudgy Ice Cream Dessert

19 ice cream sandwiches
1 (12 ounce) carton whipped topping, thawed
1 (12 ounce) jar hot fudge ice cream topping
1 cup salted peanuts, divided

- Cut 1 ice cream sandwich in half. Place 1 whole and one-half sandwich along short side of 9 x 13-inch pan. Arrange 8 sandwiches in opposite direction in pan.

- Spread with half whipped topping. Spoon teaspoonfuls of fudge topping onto whipped topping. Sprinkle with ½ cup peanuts.

- Repeat layers with remaining ice cream sandwiches, whipped topping and peanuts (pan will be full). Cover and freeze. Serves 12.

TIP: To serve, take out of freezer 20 minutes before serving.

Peanut Butter Sundae

1 cup light corn syrup
1 cup crunchy peanut butter
¼ cup milk
Ice cream or pound cake

- Stir corn syrup, peanut butter and milk in bowl until they blend well.

- Serve over ice cream or pound cake. Store in refrigerator. Serves 4.

Basic Pound Cake

1½ cups (3 sticks) butter, softened
3 cups sugar
8 eggs
3 cups sifted flour

- Preheat oven to 300°.

- Cream butter and sugar in bowl and mix well.

- Add eggs one at a time and beat well after each addition. Add flour in small amounts at a time.

- Pour into sprayed, floured 10-inch bundt pan and bake for 1 hour 30 minutes. Do not open oven door during baking. Serves 12.

Emergency Cheesecake

1 (8 ounce) package cream cheese, softened
1 (14 ounce) can sweetened condensed milk
½ cup lemon juice
1 (6 ounce) ready graham cracker piecrust

- Beat all ingredients in bowl. Pour into piecrust and refrigerate. Serves 8.

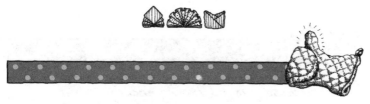

When you need a dessert in a hurry, buy a cheesecake and pour canned cherry pie filling over the top.

Butter-Pecan Cake

1 (18 ounce) box butter-pecan cake mix
½ cup (1 stick) butter, melted
1 egg
1 cup chopped pecans

- Preheat oven to 350°.

- Combine cake mix, ¾ cup water, butter and egg in bowl; beat well. Stir in pecans.

- Pour into sprayed, floured 9 x 13-inch baking dish.

- Bake as is or add pecan cake topping below before baking.

- Bake for 40 minutes or until toothpick inserted in center comes out clean. Serves 12.

Pecan Cake Topping

1 (8 ounce) package cream cheese, softened
2 eggs
1 (1 pound) box powdered sugar

- Beat cream cheese, eggs and powdered sugar in bowl. Pour over cake mixture. Yields 1 pint.

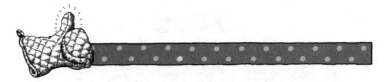

Purposely avoid having enough chairs for everyone at an informal party. This will keep guests mingling.

Oreo Cake

1 (18 ounce) box white cake mix
⅓ cup canola oil
4 egg whites
2¼ cups coarsely chopped Oreo® cookies

- Preheat oven to 350°.

- Combine cake mix, oil, 1¼ cups water and egg whites in bowl. Blend on low speed until moist. Beat for 2 minutes at high speed.

- Gently fold in 1¼ cups coarsely chopped cookies. Pour batter into 2 sprayed, floured 8-inch round cake pans.

- Bake for 25 to 30 minutes or until toothpick inserted in center comes out clean.

- Cool for 15 minutes and remove from pan. Cool completely and frost.

Oreo Cake Frosting

4¼ cups powdered sugar
1 cup (2 sticks) butter, softened
1 cup shortening (not butter-flavored)
1 teaspoon almond flavoring

- Combine all ingredients in bowl and beat until creamy.

- Frost first layer of cake and place second layer on top and frost top and sides.

- Sprinkle with remaining crushed Oreo® cookies on top. Serves 12.

Chocolate Pudding Cake

1 (18 ounce) box milk chocolate cake mix
1¼ cups milk
⅓ cup canola oil
3 eggs

- Preheat oven to 350°.

- Combine all ingredients in bowl and beat well.

- Pour into sprayed, floured 9 x 13-inch baking pan.

- Bake for 35 minutes or when toothpick inserted in center comes out clean.

Chocolate Pudding Cake Frosting

This is a very good, quick frosting on any cake.

1 (14 ounce) can sweetened condensed milk
¾ (16 ounce) can chocolate syrup
1 (8 ounce) carton whipped topping, thawed
⅓ cup chopped pecans

- Mix sweetened condensed milk and chocolate syrup in small bowl.

- Pour over cake and let soak into cake. Refrigerate for several hours.

- Spread whipped topping over top of cake and sprinkle pecans on top. Refrigerate. Serves 12.

Chocolate-Cherry Cake

1 (18 ounce) box milk chocolate cake mix
1 (20 ounce) can cherry pie filling
3 eggs

- Preheat oven to 350°.

- Combine all ingredients in bowl and mix with spoon.

- Pour into sprayed, floured 9 x 13-inch baking pan.

- Bake for 35 to 40 minutes or when toothpick inserted in center comes out clean.

Chocolate-Cherry Cake Frosting

5 tablespoons butter
1¼ cups sugar
½ cup milk
1 (6 ounce) package chocolate chips

- When cake is done, combine butter, sugar and milk in medium saucepan.

- Boil for 1 minute, stirring constantly. Add chocolate chips and stir until chips melt. Pour over hot cake. Serves 12.

The price of freedom is eternal vigilance. Thomas Jefferson

Chocolate-Orange Cake

1 (10 ounce) loaf frozen pound cake, thawed
1 (12 ounce) jar orange marmalade, divided
1 (16 ounce) can ready-to-spread chocolate fudge frosting

- Cut cake horizontally to make 3 layers.

- Place 1 layer on cake platter. Spread with half marmalade.

- Place second layer over first and spread on remaining marmalade.

- Top with third cake layer and spread frosting liberally on top and sides of cake. Refrigerate. Serves 8 to 10.

Quick Apple Cake

1 (18 ounce) box spiced cake mix
1 (20 ounce) can apple pie filling
2 eggs
⅓ cup chopped walnuts

- Preheat oven to 350°.

- Combine all ingredients in bowl and mix very thoroughly with spoon. Make sure all lumps from cake mix break up.

- Pour into sprayed, floured bundt pan. Bake for 50 minutes or when toothpick inserted in center comes out clean. Serves 10 to 12.

TIP: You may substitute any other pie filling for this cake.

Lemon-Pineapple Cake

1 (18 ounce) box lemon cake mix
1 (20 ounce) can crushed pineapple with liquid
3 eggs
⅓ cup canola oil

- Preheat oven to 350°. Combine all ingredients in bowl. Blend on low speed to moisten and beat on medium for 2 minutes.

- Pour batter into sprayed, floured 9 x 13-inch baking pan.

- Bake for 30 minutes. Cake is done when toothpick inserted in center comes out clean.

- When cake is baking, start topping for cake. Cool for about 15 minutes.

Lemon-Pineapple Cake Topping

1 (14 ounce) can sweetened condensed milk
1 cup sour cream
¼ cup lemon juice

- Combine all ingredients in medium bowl. Stir and blend well.

- Pour over cake. Refrigerate. Serves 12.

Pound cakes were named because of the equal weight of each of the ingredients: 1 pound flour, 1 pound butter, 1 pound sugar and 1 pound eggs (approximately 8 large eggs).

Chiffon Torte

1 round bakery orange chiffon cake
1 (20 ounce) can crushed pineapple with liquid
1 (5 ounce) package vanilla instant pudding
1 (8 ounce) carton whipped topping

- Slice cake horizontally to make 3 layers.

- Combine pineapple and pudding in bowl and beat with spoon until mixture begins to thicken. Fold in whipped topping.

- Spread on each layer and cover top of cake. Refrigerate overnight. Serves 12.

Easy Pineapple Cake

2 cups sugar
2 cups flour
1 (20 ounce) can crushed pineapple with liquid
1 teaspoon baking soda

- Preheat oven to 350°.

- Combine all ingredients in bowl and mix with spoon.

- Pour into sprayed, floured 9 x 13-inch baking pan. Bake for 30 to 35 minutes.

Easy Pineapple Cake Topping

1 (8 ounce) package cream cheese, softened
½ cup (1 stick) butter, melted
1 cup powdered sugar
1 cup chopped pecans

- Beat cream cheese, butter and powdered sugar in bowl

- Add chopped pecans and spoon over hot cake. Serves 12.

Fluffy Orange Cake

1 (18 ounce) box orange cake mix
4 eggs
⅔ cup canola oil

- Preheat oven to 350°. Combine all ingredients and ½ cup water in bowl.

- Beat on low speed to blend and beat on medium speed for 2 minutes. Pour into sprayed, floured 9 x 13-inch baking pan.

- Bake for 30 minutes or until toothpick inserted in center comes out clean. Cool.

Fluffy Orange Cake Topping

1 (14 ounce) can sweetened condensed milk
⅓ cup lemon juice
1 (8 ounce) carton whipped topping
2 (11 ounce) cans mandarin oranges, drained, halved, chilled

- Blend sweetened condensed milk and lemon juice in large bowl and mix well.

- Fold in whipped topping until blended well. Fold in orange slices.

- Pour mixture over cooled cake. Cover and refrigerate. Serves 12.

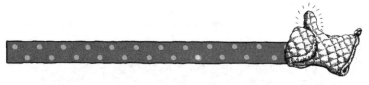

Fat-free half-and-half cream works just as well as half-and-half cream. There's no difference in taste or texture when used in a recipe.

Hawaiian Dream Cake

1 (18 ounce) box yellow cake mix
4 eggs
¾ cup canola oil
½ (20 ounce) can crushed pineapple with ½ liquid

- Preheat oven to 350°.

- Beat all ingredients in bowl for 4 minutes.

- Pour into sprayed, floured 9 x 13-inch baking pan.

- Bake for 30 to 35 minutes or until toothpick inserted in center comes out clean.

Coconut Pineapple Glaze

This glaze is great on Hawaiian Dream Cake.

½ (20 ounce) can crushed pineapple with ½ liquid (left from
    cake ingredients)
½ cup (1 stick) butter
1 (16 ounce) box powdered sugar
1 (7 ounce) can flaked coconut

- Heat pineapple and butter in saucepan and boil for 1½ minutes.

- Add powdered sugar and coconut.

- Punch holes in cake with knife. Pour hot icing over cake. Refrigerate. Serves 12.

You can't change the past, but you can ruin the present by worrying over the future. Anonymous

Pound Cake Deluxe

1 (10 inch) round bakery pound cake
1 (20 ounce) can crushed pineapple with liquid
1 (5 ounce) package coconut instant pudding mix
1 (8 ounce) carton whipped topping

- Slice cake horizontally to make 3 layers. Mix pineapple, pudding and whipped topping in bowl and blend well.

- Spread on each layer and top of cake. Refrigerate. Serves 12.

Coconut-Angel Cake

1 (14 ounce/10 inch) round angel food cake
1 (20 ounce) can coconut pie filling
1 (12 ounce) carton whipped topping
3 tablespoons flaked coconut

- Cut angel food cake horizontally to make 3 layers.

- Combine coconut pie filling and whipped topping. Spread one-third mixture on first layer. Top with second layer.

- Spread one-third mixture on second layer and top with third layer. Spread remaining whipped topping mixture on top of cake.

- Sprinkle coconut on top of cake. Refrigerate. Serves 12.

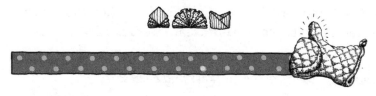

Grandmas are moms with lots of frosting. Author Unknown

Strawberry Delight

1 (6 ounce) package strawberry gelatin
2 (10 ounce) packages frozen strawberries with juice
1 (8 ounce) carton whipped topping
1 (12 ounce) prepared angel food cake

- Dissolve strawberry gelatin in 1 cup boiling water in bowl and mix well. Add strawberries.

- Refrigerate until partially set and fold in whipped topping.

- Break angel food cake into large bite-size pieces and layer cake and gelatin mixture in 9 x 13-inch shallow dish.

- Refrigerate. Cut in squares to serve. Serves 12.

Pink Lady Cake

1 (18 ounce) box strawberry cake mix
3 eggs
1 teaspoon lemon extract
1 (20 ounce) can strawberry pie filling

- Preheat oven to 350°.

- Beat cake mix, eggs and lemon extract in bowl. Fold into pie filling.

- Pour in sprayed, floured 9 x 13-inch baking pan.

- Bake for 30 to 35 minutes. Cake is done when toothpick inserted in center comes out clean. Serves 12.

TIP: *If you want an icing, try a prepared vanilla frosting or whipped topping. They are the quickest and easiest.*

Angel Glaze for Cakes

1 cup powdered sugar
2 tablespoons light corn syrup
¼ teaspoon vanilla

- Mix all ingredients with 1 tablespoon water in bowl and stir until blended well.

- Glaze should pour slowly and stay on cake long enough to soak in. If glaze runs down side of cake, thicken mixture with a little more powdered sugar.

- Use on any cake that needs light icing or topping of something sweet. Yields glaze for 1 cake.

Easy Apricot-Chiffon Pie

2 (6 ounce) cartons apricot-mango yogurt
1 (3 ounce) box apricot gelatin
1 (8 ounce) carton whipped topping
1 (6 ounce) ready shortbread piecrust

- Combine yogurt and dry gelatin in bowl and mix well.

- Fold in whipped topping, spread in piecrust and freeze.

- Take out of freezer 20 minutes before slicing. Serves 6.

TIP: *This is an easy pie to duplicate using your favorite yogurt flavors with gelatin flavors. When you fold in anything with whipped topping it's going to be good.*

Magic Cherry Pie

2 (6 ounce) cartons cherry yogurt
1 (3 ounce) package dry cherry gelatin
1 (8 ounce) carton whipped topping, thawed
1 (6 ounce) ready shortbread piecrust

- Combine yogurt and dry gelatin in bowl and mix well.

- Fold in whipped topping and spoon into piecrust.

- Freeze. Take out of freezer 20 minutes before slicing. Serves 8.

TIP: Just add several spoonfuls of cherry pie filling on top of this pie and it will be even better.

Creamy Cherry-Lime Pie

2 (8 ounce) cartons lime yogurt
⅓ cup chopped maraschino cherries, divided
1 (8 ounce) carton whipped topping, thawed
1 (6 ounce) ready graham cracker piecrust

- Stir yogurt and ¼ cup cherries in bowl. Fold in whipped topping.

- Spoon mixture into piecrust and garnish with chopped cherries. Refrigerate for 6 to 8 hours or until firm. Serves 8.

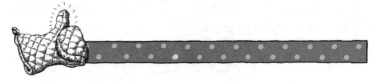

Have old memories, but young hopes.

Guiltless Limeade Pie

1 (6 ounce) can frozen limeade concentrate, thawed
2 cups low-fat frozen yogurt, softened
1 (8 ounce) carton whipped topping, thawed
1 (6 ounce) ready graham cracker piecrust

• Combine limeade concentrate and yogurt in large bowl and mix well. Fold in whipped topping.

• Pour into piecrust. Freeze for at least 4 hours or overnight. Serves 6.

Frozen Lemonade Pie

½ gallon frozen yogurt, softened
1 (6 ounce) can frozen pink lemonade concentrate, thawed
1 (6 ounce) ready graham cracker piecrust
1 (8 ounce) carton frozen whipped topping, thawed

• Combine frozen yogurt and pink lemonade concentrate in large bowl. Work quickly.

• Pile mixture into piecrust and freeze.

• Top with layer of whipped topping before serving. Serves 8.

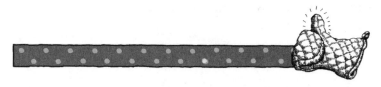

By the time you learn the rules of life, you're too old to play the game.

Creamy Lime-Almond Pie

2 cups almond shortbread cookie crumbs, divided
½ cup (1 stick) butter, softened
1 cup lime sherbet, softened
1 cup whipped topping, thawed

- Preheat oven to 350°.

- Mix 1½ cups cookie crumbs with butter and pat evenly into 9-inch pie pan.

- Bake for 10 minutes, remove and cool.

- Combine sherbet and whipped topping in bowl. Place in crumb crust and sprinkle remaining cookie crumbs on top.

- Refrigerate for 6 to 8 hours or until firm. Serves 8.

Five-Citrus Cream Pie

1 (4 ounce) can sweetened condensed milk
1 (6 ounce) can frozen five-citrus concentrate, partially thawed
1 (8 ounce) carton whipped topping, thawed
1 (6 ounce) ready graham cracker piecrust

- Stir sweetened condensed milk and five-citrus concentrate in bowl until they mix well.

- Fold into whipped topping. Spoon mixture into piecrust. Refrigerate for 6 to 8 hours. Serves 8.

Pineapple-Fluff Pie

1 (20 ounce) can crushed pineapple with liquid
1 (3.4 ounce) package instant lemon pudding mix
1 (8 ounce) carton whipped topping
1 (6 ounce) ready graham cracker piecrust

- Combine pineapple and pudding mix in bowl and beat until it thickens.

- Fold in whipped topping. Spoon into piecrust.

- Refrigerate for several hours before serving. Serves 8.

Easy Pumpkin Pie

2 eggs
1 (30 ounce) can pumpkin pie mix
1 (5 ounce) can evaporated milk
1 (9 inch) deep-dish piecrust

- Preheat oven to 400°.

- Beat eggs lightly in large bowl. Stir in pumpkin pie mix and evaporated milk. Pour mixture into piecrust.

- Cut 2-inch strips of foil and cover crust edges to prevent excessive browning.

- Bake for 15 minutes. Reduce temperature to 325° and bake for additional 40 minutes or until knife inserted in center comes out clean. Cool. Serves 8.

Four-Step Strawberry Pie

1 (6 ounce) box strawberry gelatin
1 (6 ounce) ready graham cracker piecrust
2 (10 ounce) packages frozen strawberries
1 (8 ounce) carton whipped topping

- Combine gelatin and ¾ cup boiling water in bowl and mix well.

- Cool gelatin in refrigerator until it begins to thicken. (Watch closely.) Spoon into piecrust.

- Drain 1 package strawberries and fold whipped topping into 1 package drained and 1 package undrained strawberries. Spoon into piecrust.

- Refrigerate for several hours before serving. Serves 8.

Very Berry Pie

1 (6 ounce) package strawberry gelatin
1 (16 ounce) can whole cranberry sauce
1 (8 ounce) carton whipped topping, thawed
1 (6 ounce) ready graham cracker piecrust

- Dissolve gelatin in ¾ cup boiling water. Add cranberry sauce. Place in refrigerator until it thickens.

- Fold in whipped topping and pour into piecrust. Refrigerate for several hours before serving. Serves 8.

TIP: If the gelatin-cranberry sauce mixture gets a little too thick you can add ½ cup cranberry juice to thin it before you chill it the final time.

Peaches 'n Cream Pie

1 (15 ounce) jar chocolate syrup
1 (6 ounce) ready shortbread piecrust
1 quart peach ice cream, softened
Fresh peach slices

- Drizzle ½ cup chocolate syrup over bottom of piecrust. Spoon ice cream over crust and freeze for 3 hours or until firm.

- When ready to serve, place peach slices over top of ice cream. Drizzle with additional chocolate syrup. Serves 6.

Cool Chocolate Pie

22 large marshmallows
3 (5 ounce) milk chocolate-almond candy bars
1 (8 ounce) carton whipped topping
1 (6 ounce) ready graham cracker piecrust

- Melt marshmallows and chocolate bars in double boiler. Cool partially and fold in whipped topping.

- Pour into piecrust. Refrigerate for several hours before serving. Serves 6.

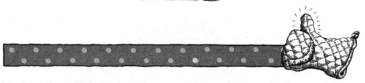

Peaches are a great source of vitamin C and fiber. One peach provides 10% of the daily requirement of vitamin C and 8% of the daily requirement of fiber.

Mint-Chocolate Pie

1 cup mint-chocolate chip ice cream, softened
1 cup whipped topping, thawed
¾ cup crushed chocolate sandwich cookies with mint filling,
   divided
1 (6 ounce) ready chocolate cookie piecrust

- Combine ice cream, whipping topping and ½ cup crushed
  cookies in bowl.

- Place in piecrust and sprinkle remaining cookie crumbs on top.

- Freeze for 3 to 4 hours or until firm. Serves 8.

Creme de Mint Lament

22 large marshmallows
⅓ cup creme de menthe liqueur
1½ cups whipping cream, whipped
1 (6 ounce) ready chocolate piecrust

- Melt marshmallows with creme de menthe in large saucepan
  over low heat and cool.

- Fold whipped cream into marshmallow mixture.

- Pour filling into piecrust and freeze until ready to serve. Serves 8.

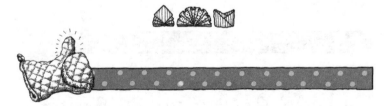

*The victor will never be asked if he told
the truth.* Adolf Hitler

Irresistible Chocolate-Amaretto Pie

3 (5 ounce) milk chocolate-almond candy bars
⅓ cup amaretto liqueur
2 (8 ounce) cartons whipping cream, whipped
1 (6 ounce) ready shortbread piecrust

- Melt chocolate in double boiler on low heat. Remove from heat and pour in amaretto.

- Stir chocolate and amaretto for about 10 or 15 minutes until mixture reaches room temperature.

- Fold in whipped cream. Pour into piecrust. Refrigerate for several hours before serving. Serves 8.

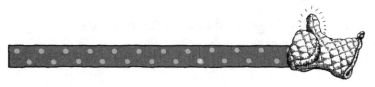

For many of the desserts in this cookbook, you can add a topping of some kind to introduce more flavors. It's a good idea to keep a can of pie filling in your pantry and whipped topping in your freezer.

Other toppings include ice cream, nuts, honey, chocolate syrup, powdered sugar, fruit and many others. If you want to be creative, here's your chance!

Easy Chocolate Pie

2 (5 ounce) milk chocolate candy bars
1 (16 ounce) carton frozen whipped topping, thawed, divided
¾ cup chopped pecans
1 (9 inch) frozen piecrust, cooked

• Break candy into small pieces and melt in saucepan over low heat. Remove and cool for several minutes.

• Fold in two-thirds whipped topping and mix well. Stir in chopped pecans and pour into piecrust.

• Spread remaining whipped topping over top of pie. Refrigerate for at least 8 hours. Serves 8.

Caramel Ice Cream Pie

1 (18 ounce) roll refrigerated butterscotch cookies
½ gallon vanilla ice cream
1 (12 ounce) jar caramel ice cream topping

• Bake cookies according to package directions.

• When cookies cool, crumble and place in 10-inch deep-dish pie pan, but set aside about ½ cup crumbs to use for topping.

• Place ice cream in bowl to soften. Stir caramel sauce into ice cream (do not mix completely) and spoon mixture into pie pan.

• Sprinkle remaining crumbs over top of pie and freeze. Serves 8.

Million-Dollar Pie

24 round, buttery crackers, crumbled
1 cup chopped pecans
4 egg whites (absolutely no yolks at all)
1 cup sugar

- Preheat oven to 350°.

- Mix cracker crumbs with pecans in bowl.

- In separate bowl, beat egg whites until stiff and slowly add sugar while still mixing.

- Gently fold crumbs and pecan mixture into egg whites. Pour into pie pan and bake for 20 minutes. Cool before serving. Serves 6.

Cream Cheese Crust

Use with any pie filling.

½ cup (1 stick) butter, softened
1 (3 ounce) package cream cheese, softened
1 cup flour

- Beat butter, cream cheese and flour in bowl.

- Blend with pastry blender or with fork until mixture can be made into ball. Refrigerate pastry for 1 hour.

- Roll out on floured surface to 9-inch round. Place inside 9-inch pie pan and press down evenly. Yields 1 (9 inch) piecrust.

TIP: *Fill crust with your favorite pie filling and top with whipped topping, nuts or fruit slices.*

Three-Step Blueberry Cobbler

2 (20 ounce) cans blueberry pie filling
1 (18 ounce) box white cake mix
1 egg
½ cup (1 stick) butter, softened

- Preheat oven to 350°.

- Spread pie filling in sprayed 9 x 13-inch baking dish.

- Combine cake mix, egg and butter in bowl and blend well. Mixture will be stiff. Spoon filling over top.

- Bake for 45 minutes or until golden brown. Serves 12 to 14.

Quickie Cherry Crisp

2 (20 ounce) cans cherry pie filling
1 (18 ounce) box white cake mix
½ cup (1 stick) butter
2 cups chopped pecans

- Preheat oven to 350°.

- Pour pie filling into sprayed 10 x 15-inch baking dish.

- Sprinkle cake mix over top of filling. Dot with butter and cover with pecans.

- Bake for 45 minutes. Serves 12.

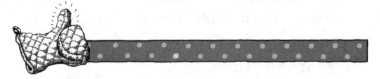

A good example is the best sermon.
Anonymous

Choice Peach Crunch

2 (20 ounce) cans peach pie filling
1 (18 ounce) box white cake mix
1 cup slivered almonds
½ cup (1 stick) butter

- Preheat oven to 350°.

- Add pie filling evenly in sprayed, floured 9 x 13-inch baking pan.

- Sprinkle cake mix evenly and smooth over top. Sprinkle almonds evenly over cake mix.

- Slice butter into ⅛-inch slices and place over entire surface.

- Bake for 40 to 45 minutes or until top is brown. Serves 12 to 14.

Mom's Brown Sugar Cookies

¾ cup packed brown sugar
1 cup (2 sticks) butter, softened
1 egg yolk
2 cups flour

- Cream brown sugar and butter in bowl until light and fluffy. Mix in egg yolk. Blend in flour. Refrigerate dough for 1 hour.

- When ready to bake, preheat oven to 325°.

- Form dough into 1-inch balls, flatten and criss-cross with fork on lightly sprayed cookie sheet.

- Bake for 10 to 12 minutes or until golden brown. Yields 2 dozen.

Butter Cookie Special

1 (18 ounce) box butter cake mix
1 (3.4 ounce) package butterscotch instant pudding mix
1 cup canola oil
1 egg, beaten

- Preheat oven to 350°.

- Combine cake mix, pudding mix, oil and egg in bowl and mix with spoon. Beat thoroughly.

- Drop teaspoonfuls of dough onto cookie sheet about 2 inches apart.

- Bake for about 8 minutes. Do not overcook. Yields 3 dozen.

Yummy Butter Cookies

1 pound (4 sticks) butter
¾ cup packed brown sugar
¾ cup sugar
4½ cups flour

- Preheat oven to 350°.

- Cream butter, brown sugar and sugar in bowl, slowly add flour and mix well. (Batter will be very thick.)

- Roll into small balls and place onto cookie sheet.

- Bake for about 15 minutes until only slightly brown. Do not over bake. Yields 3 dozen.

Creamy Cheesecake Cookies

1 cup (2 sticks) butter, softened
2 (3 ounce) packages cream cheese, softened
2 cups sugar
2 cups flour

- Preheat oven to 325°.

- Beat butter and cream cheese in bowl. Add sugar and beat until light and fluffy. Add flour and beat well.

- Drop teaspoonfuls of dough onto cookie sheet and bake for 12 to 15 minutes or until edges are golden. Yields 3 dozen.

Oma's Gingerbread Cookies

¾ cup (1½ sticks) butter, softened
2 egg yolks
1 (18 ounce) box spice cake mix
1 teaspoon ginger

- Preheat oven to 375°.

- Combine butter and egg yolks in large bowl. Gradually blend in cake mix and ginger and mix well.

- Roll out to ⅛-inch (3 mm) thickness on lightly floured surface. Use gingerbread cookie cutter to cut out cookies and place 2 inches apart on cookie sheet.

- Bake for about 8 minutes or until edges are slightly brown. Cool cookies before transferring to cookie bowl. Yields 1 to 2 dozen.

Scotch Shortbread

½ cup (1 stick) butter, softened
⅓ cup sugar
1¼ cups flour
Powdered sugar

- Preheat oven to 325°.

- Cream butter and sugar in bowl until light and fluffy. Add flour and pinch of salt and mix well.

- Spread dough in 8-inch square pan. Bake for 20 minutes or until light brown.

- Cool shortbread in pan, dust with powdered sugar and cut into squares. Yields 2 dozen.

Devil's Food Cookies

1 (18 ounce) box devil's food cake mix
½ cup canola oil
2 eggs
¾ cup chopped pecans

- Preheat oven to 350°.

- Combine cake mix, oil, eggs and pecans in bowl and mix well.

- Drop teaspoonfuls of dough onto non-stick cookie sheet.

- Bake for 10 to 12 minutes. Cool and remove to wire rack. Yields 3 dozen.

Nutty Fudgies

1 (18 ounce) box fudge cake mix
1 (8 ounce) carton sour cream
⅔ cup peanut butter chips
½ cup chopped peanuts

- Preheat oven to 350°.

- Beat cake mix and sour cream in bowl until mixture blends and smooth. Stir in peanut butter chips and peanuts.

- Drop teaspoonfuls of dough onto sprayed cookie sheet. Bake for 10 to 12 minutes. Remove from oven and cool. Yields 3 dozen.

Chocolate-Crunch Cookies

1 (18 ounce) box German chocolate cake mix with pudding
1 egg, slightly beaten
½ cup (1 stick) butter, melted
1 cup rice crispy cereal

- Preheat oven to 350°.

- Combine cake mix, egg and butter in bowl. Add cereal and stir until they blend well.

- Shape dough into 1-inch balls. Place onto sprayed cookie sheet.

- Dip fork in flour and flatten cookies in crisscross pattern. Bake for 10 to 12 minutes. Cool. Yields 3 dozen.

Double Chocolate Cookies

6 egg whites
3 cups powdered sugar
¼ cup cocoa
3½ cups finely chopped pecans

- Preheat oven to 325°.

- Beat egg whites in bowl until light and frothy. Fold powdered sugar and cocoa into egg whites and beat lightly. Fold in pecans.

- Drop teaspoonfuls of dough onto sprayed, floured cookie sheet.

- Bake for about 20 minutes. Do not over bake and cool completely before removing from cookie sheet. Yields 3 dozen.

Peppy Peanut Butter Cups

1 (18 ounce) roll refrigerated peanut butter cookie dough
48 miniature peanut butter cup candies

- Preheat oven to 350°.

- Slice cookie dough into ¾-inch slices. Cut each slice into quarters and place each quarter, pointed side up in sprayed miniature muffin cups.

- Bake for 10 minutes. Remove from oven and immediately press peanut butter cup candy gently and evenly into cookies. (Be sure you take wrappers off peanut butter cups.)

- Cool and remove from pan and refrigerate until firm. Yields 48.

Chocolate-Peanut Butter Crisps

1 (10 count) package 8-inch flour tortillas
1 (8 ounce) package semi-sweet chocolate chips
⅓ cup creamy or crunchy peanut butter
1 (14 ounce) can sweetened condensed milk

- Preheat oven to 350°.

- Cut flour tortillas into 8 wedges and place on baking sheet. Bake for 10 minutes and cool on rack.

- Melt chocolate in heavy saucepan over low heat and stir constantly.

- Stir in peanut putter, sweetened condensed milk and 2 tablespoons water and heat thoroughly. (If sauce is too thick, add 1 teaspoon water at a time, until sauce smoothly drizzles on foil.)

- Drizzle warm chocolate sauce over wedges or serve immediately in chafing dish or fondue pot and dip with crisp tortilla wedges. Yields 15 to 20.

Peanut Butter Cookies

1 cup sugar
¾ cup light corn syrup
1 (16 ounce) jar crunchy peanut butter
4½ cups chow mein noodles

- Bring sugar and corn syrup in saucepan over medium heat to a boil and stir in peanut butter.

- Remove from heat and stir in noodles.

- Drop spoonfuls of dough onto wax paper and allow to cool. Yields 2 dozen.

Lemon Cookies

½ cup (1 stick) butter, softened
1 cup sugar
2 tablespoons lemon juice
2 cups flour

- Preheat oven to 350°.

- Cream butter, sugar and lemon juice in bowl and slowly stir in flour.

- Drop teaspoonfuls of dough onto cookie sheet. Bake for 14 to 15 minutes. Yields 2 dozen.

Angel Macaroons

1 (16 ounce) package 1-step angel food cake mix
1½ teaspoons almond extract
2 cups flaked coconut

- Preheat oven to 350°.

- Beat cake mix, ½ cup water and extract in bowl on low speed for 30 seconds.

- Scrape bowl, beat on medium for 1 minute and fold in coconut.

- Drop rounded teaspoonfuls of dough onto cookie sheet.

- Bake for 10 to 12 minutes or until set. Remove paper with cookies to wire rack to cool. Yields 2 dozen.

Coconut Macaroons

2 (7 ounce) packages flaked coconut
1 (14 ounce) can sweetened condensed milk
2 teaspoons vanilla
½ teaspoon almond extract

- Preheat oven to 350°.

- Combine coconut, sweetened condensed milk, vanilla and almond extract in bowl and mix well.

- Drop rounded teaspoonfuls of dough onto foil-lined cookie sheet.

- Bake for 8 to 10 minutes or until light brown around edges. Immediately remove from foil. (Macaroons will stick if allowed to cool.)

- Store at room temperature. Yields 2 dozen.

Lemon-Coconut Macaroons

⅔ cup sweetened condensed milk
1 large egg white
2 teaspoons lemon juice
3½ cups shredded sweetened coconut

- Preheat oven to 325°.

- Mix sweetened condensed milk, egg white and lemon juice in bowl and stir in coconut.

- Drop teaspoonfuls of dough 2 inches apart on cookie sheet.

- Bake for 20 minutes or until light brown. Cool completely and remove carefully. Yields 3 dozen.

No-Cook Lemon Balls

2½ cups graham cracker crumbs, divided
1 (6 ounce) can frozen lemonade concentrate, thawed
½ cup (1 stick) butter, softened
1 (16 ounce) box powdered sugar, sifted

- Combine 1½ cups cracker crumbs, lemonade concentrate, butter and powdered sugar in bowl. Shape into small balls.

- Roll in reserved cracker crumbs and put on wax paper.

- Refrigerate for 3 to 4 hours in airtight container or freeze to serve later. Yields 3 dozen.

TIP: *You can substitute almond or pecan shortbread cookie crumbs instead of graham cracker crumbs.*

Light Pecan Puffs

2 egg whites
¾ cup packed light brown sugar
1 teaspoon vanilla
1 cup chopped pecans

- Preheat oven to 250°.

- Beat egg whites in bowl until foamy. Gradually add (¼ cup at a time) brown sugar and vanilla.

- Continue beating until stiff peaks form (about 3 or 4 minutes). Fold in pecans.

- Drop teaspoonfuls of mixture onto cookie sheet. Bake for 45 minutes. Yields 2 dozen.

Morning Meringues

¾ cup sugar
2 egg whites, beaten stiff
1 cup chopped nuts
1 cup chocolate chips

- Preheat oven to 350°.

- Add sugar to stiffly beaten egg whites in bowl. Add nuts and chocolate chips.

- Line cookie sheet with foil. Drop teaspoonfuls of mixture and press down.

- Bake for 10 minutes. Turn oven off. Let cookies sit in oven for 8 to 10 hours. Yields 2 dozen.

Sweet Walnut Bars

1⅔ cups graham cracker crumbs
1½ cups coarsely chopped walnuts
1 (14 ounce) can sweetened condensed milk
¼ cup flaked coconut, optional

- Preheat oven to 350°.

- Place graham cracker crumbs and walnuts in bowl. Slowly add sweetened condensed milk, coconut and pinch of salt. Mixture will be very thick.

- Pack into sprayed 9-inch square pan. Pack mixture down with back of spoon.

- Bake for 35 minutes. When cool cut into squares. Serves 9 to 12.

Chocolate Chip-Cheese Bars

1 (18 ounce) tube refrigerated chocolate chip cookie dough
1 (8 ounce) package cream cheese, softened
½ cup sugar
1 egg

- Preheat oven to 325°.

- Cut cookie dough half. For crust, press half dough onto bottom of sprayed 9-inch square baking pan or 7 x 11-inch baking pan.

- Beat cream cheese, sugar and egg in bowl until smooth. Spread over crust. Crumble remaining dough over top.

- Bake for 35 to 40 minutes or until toothpick inserted in center comes out clean. Cool on wire rack. Cut into bars. Refrigerate leftovers. Serves 12.

Special Apricot Bars

1¼ cups flour
¾ cup packed brown sugar
6 tablespoons (¾ stick) butter
¾ cup apricot preserves

- Preheat oven to 350°.

- Combine flour, brown sugar and butter in bowl and mix well.

- Place half mixture in 9-inch square baking pan. Spread apricot preserves over top of mixture. Add remaining flour mixture over top of dessert.

- Bake for 30 minutes. Cut into squares. Yields 1 dozen.

Chocolate-Cherry Bars

1 (18 ounce) box devils food cake mix
1 (20 ounce) can cherry pie filling
2 eggs
1 cup milk chocolate chips

- Preheat oven to 350°.

- Mix all ingredients in large bowl with spoon and blend well.

- Pour batter into sprayed, floured 9 x 13-inch baking dish.

- Bake for 25 to 30 minutes or until toothpick inserted in center comes out clean. Cool and frost.

Chocolate-Cherry Bars Frosting

3 (1 ounce) square semi-sweet chocolate, melted
1 (3 ounce) package cream cheese, softened
½ teaspoon vanilla
1½ cups powdered sugar

- Beat chocolate, cream cheese and vanilla in medium bowl until smooth. Gradually beat in powdered sugar.

- Pour over chocolate-cherry bars. Yields 1½ dozen.

How do you identify an "authentic" peanut butter cookie? By the criss-cross design on the top, of course! This practice dates back to a 1931 edition of Pillsbury's "Balanced Recipes," which included "Peanut Butter Balls" flattened with a fork. Even today's cooks wouldn't think of skipping this time-honored tradition.

Nutty Blonde Brownies

1 (1 pound) box light brown sugar
4 eggs
2 cups biscuit mix
2 cups chopped pecans

- Preheat oven to 350°.

- Beat brown sugar, eggs and biscuit mix in bowl. Stir in pecans and pour into sprayed 9 x 13-inch baking pan.

- Bake for 35 minutes. Cool and cut into squares. Yields 1½ dozen.

Secret Snickers Brownies

1 (18 ounce) box German chocolate cake mix
¾ cup (1½ sticks) butter, melted
½ cup evaporated milk
4 (3 ounce) Snickers® candy bars, cut in ⅛-inch slices

- Preheat oven to 350°.

- Combine cake mix, butter and evaporated milk in large bowl. Beat on low speed until mixture blends well.

- Add half batter into sprayed, floured 9 x 13-inch baking pan. Bake for 10 minutes.

- Remove from oven and place candy bar slices evenly over brownies. Drop spoonfuls of remaining batter over candy bars and spread as evenly as possible.

- Place back in oven and bake for additional 20 minutes. When cool, cut into squares. Yields 1½ dozen.

Best Butterscotch Bites

1 (12 ounce) and 1 (6 ounce) package butterscotch chips
2¼ cups chow mein noodles
½ cup chopped walnuts
¼ cup flaked coconut

- Melt butterscotch chips in double boiler. Add noodles, walnuts and coconut.

- Drop tablespoonfuls of mixture onto wax paper. Yields 2 dozen.

Salty Haystacks

1 (12 ounce) package butterscotch chips
1 cup salted peanuts
1½ cups chow mein noodles

- Melt butterscotch chips in double boiler. Remove from heat and stir in peanuts and noodles.

- Drop teaspoonfuls of mixture onto wax paper.

- Cool and store in airtight container. Yields 2 dozen.

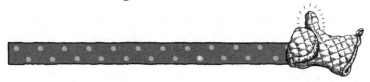

George Washington Carver is the father of the peanut industry because of his research begun in 1903 at Tuskegee Institute. He discovered and developed more than 300 uses for peanuts. He also convinced Southern farmers that peanuts could be a cash crop and planted as a rotation crop. Agriculture in the South changed forever.

Peanutty Cocoa Puffs

¾ cup light corn syrup
1¼ cups sugar
1¼ cups crunchy peanut butter
4½ cups cocoa puff cereal

- Bring syrup and sugar in large saucepan to a rolling boil. Stir in peanut butter and mix well. Stir in cocoa puffs.

- Drop teaspoonfuls of mixture onto wax paper. Yields 3 dozen.

Scotch Crunchies

½ cup crunchy peanut butter
1 (6 ounce) package butterscotch chips
2½ cups frosted flakes cereal
½ cup peanuts

- Combine peanut butter and butterscotch chips in large saucepan and melt over low heat.

- Stir until butterscotch chips and melt. Stir in cereal and peanuts.

- Drop teaspoonfuls of mixture onto wax paper. Refrigerate until firm. Store in airtight container. Yields 2 dozen.

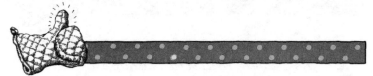

Peanuts contain healthy monounsaturated fats as well as vitamin E, folic acid, magnesium, copper, fiber and plant proteins. They are naturally cholesterol-free, help to control blood cholesterol levels and have almost none of the bad trans fats.

Perky Pecan Squares

1 (24 ounce) package almond bark
1 cup cinnamon chips
1 cup chopped pecans
8 cups frosted rice crispy cereal

- Melt almond bark and cinnamon chips in very large saucepan or roasting pan on low heat and stir constantly.

- After it melts, remove from heat and add pecans and frosted crispy rice cereal.

- Mix well and stir into 9 x 13-inch pan. Pat down with back of spoon. Refrigerate just until set. Cut into squares. Yields 1½ dozen.

Old-Fashioned Marshmallow Treats

¼ cup (½ stick) butter
4 cups miniature marshmallows
½ cup crunchy peanut butter
5 cups rice crispy cereal

- Melt butter in saucepan on medium heat and add marshmallows. Stir until they melt and add peanut butter.

- Remove from heat. Add cereal and stir well. Press mixture into 9 x 13-inch pan. Cut in squares when cool. Yields 1½ dozen.

Cocoa Chocolate Bites

1 (12 ounce) package milk chocolate chips
⅔ cup crunchy peanut butter
4¼ cups cocoa-flavored, rice crispy cereal

- Melt chocolate chips in double boiler, stir in peanut butter and stir in cereal.

- Press into 9-inch square pan and let stand for 1 hour. Cut into squares. Yields 1 dozen.

Nuthouse Chocolate Fudge

1 (12 ounce) package white chocolate chips
¾ cup hazelnut-cocoa spread
1½ cups chopped hazelnuts, divided

- Melt white chocolate chips and add hazelnut spread in medium saucepan over low heat.

- Cook and stir until mixture blends well.

- Remove from heat and stir in 1 cup hazelnuts.

- Drop teaspoonfuls of mixture onto wax paper. Garnish with reserved hazelnuts. Refrigerate until set. Yields 2 dozen.

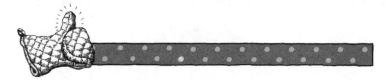

By law peanut butter must be composed of at least 90% peanuts. If the percentage is less, the product is called peanut spread.

Diamond Lil's Fudge

1 (6 ounce) package semi-sweet chocolate chips
1 cup peanut butter
½ cup (1 stick) butter
1 cup powdered sugar

- Cook chocolate chips, peanut butter and butter in saucepan over low heat, stirring constantly, just until mixture melts and is smooth. Remove from heat.

- Add powdered sugar and stir until smooth.

- Spoon into sprayed 8-inch square pan and refrigerate until firm. Cut into squares. Yields 1 dozen.

Chunky Peanut Butter Fudge

1½ cups crunchy peanut butter
1 (12 ounce) package milk chocolate chips
1 (14 ounce) can sweetened condensed milk
1 cup chopped pecans

- Combine peanut butter and chocolate chips and sweetened condensed milk in saucepan. Heat on low, stirring constantly, until chocolate melts.

- Add pecans and mix well. Pour into sprayed 9 x 9-inch pan. Cut into squares. Yields 1½ dozen.

A man who never made a mistake, never made anything. Anonymous

Sweet Raisin Fudge

1 (12 ounce) package semi-sweet chocolate chips
1 cup crunchy peanut butter
3 cups miniature marshmallows
¾ cup raisins

- Melt chocolate chips and peanut butter in saucepan over medium-low heat.

- Fold in marshmallows and raisins and stir until marshmallows melt. Pour into 7 x 11-inch pan.

- Refrigerate until firm. Cut into squares. Store where it is cool. Yields 1 dozen.

Microwave Fudge Zap

3 cups semi-sweet chocolate chips
1 (14 ounce) can sweetened condensed milk
¼ cup (½ stick) butter, cut into pieces
1 cup chopped walnuts

- Combine chocolate chips, sweetened condensed milk and butter in 2-quart glass bowl.

- Microwave on MEDIUM for 4 to 5 minutes and stir at 1½-minute intervals.

- Stir in walnuts and pour into sprayed 8-inch square dish. Refrigerate for 2 hours. Cut into squares. Yields 1 dozen.

Quick Chewy Pralines

1 (3 ounce) box butterscotch cook-and-serve pudding
1¼ cups sugar
½ cup evaporated milk
2 cups pecan pieces

- Combine butterscotch pudding, sugar and milk in large saucepan.

- Bring to a boil, stirring constantly, for 2 minutes.

- Add pecans, boil for additional 1½ minutes and stir constantly.

- Remove from heat. Beat until candy begins to cool and drop tablespoonfuls of mixture onto wax paper. Yields 2 dozen.

Yummy Pralines

½ cup (1 stick) butter
1 (16 ounce) box light brown sugar
1 (8 ounce) carton whipping cream
2½ cups pecan halves

- Combine butter, brown sugar and whipping cream in heavy saucepan.

- Cook until temperature comes to soft-ball stage (about 20 minutes) and stir constantly. Remove from heat and set aside for 5 minutes.

- Fold in pecans and stir until ingredients are glassy looking. (This will take several minutes of stirring.)

- Drop tablespoonfuls of mixture onto wax paper. Remove after pralines cool. Yields 2 dozen.

Super Chocolate Toffee

1 cup sugar
1 cup (2 sticks) butter
1 (6 ounce) package chocolate chips
1 cup chopped pecans

- Combine sugar and butter in heavy saucepan. Cook until candy reaches hard-crack stage. Pour onto sprayed 7 x 11-inch dish.

- Melt chocolate in double boiler and spread over toffee.

- Sprinkle with pecans and press pecans into chocolate.

- Refrigerate briefly to set chocolate. Break into pieces. Yields 1 dozen.

Jiffy Macadamia Candy

2 (3 ounce) jars macadamia nuts
1 (20 ounce) package white almond bark
¾ cup flaked coconut

- Heat dry skillet and toast nuts until slightly golden. (Some brands of macadamia nuts are already toasted.) Set aside.

- Melt 12 squares almond bark in double boiler.

- As soon as almond bark melts, pour in macadamia nuts and coconut and stir well.

- Place wax paper on cookie sheet, pour candy onto wax paper and spread out. Refrigerate for 30 minutes to set. Break into pieces. Yields 2 dozen.

In-Your-Dreams Candy

2 (8 ounce) cartons whipping cream
3 cups sugar
1 cup light corn syrup
1 cup chopped pecans

- Combine whipping cream, sugar and corn syrup in saucepan. Cook to soft-boil stage.

- Stir and beat until candy cools.

- Add pecans and pour into sprayed 9-inch pan. Cut into squares. Yields 1 to 1½ dozen.

Holiday Date Loaf Candy

3 cups sugar
1 cup milk
1 (16 ounce) box chopped dates
1 cup chopped pecans

- Combine sugar and milk in large saucepan.

- Cook to soft-boil stage (235° on candy thermometer). Stir in dates. Cook to hard boil stage (260°), stirring constantly.

- Remove from heat, add pecans and mix well. Stir and cool until stiff. Pour mixture onto damp tea towel.

- Roll into log. Let stand until set. When candy is set, remove tea towel and slice. Yields 2 dozen.

Almond-Peanut Clusters

1 (24 ounce) package almond bark
1 (12 ounce) package milk chocolate chips
5 cups salted peanuts

- Melt almond bark and chocolate chips in double boiler.

- Stir in peanuts and drop teaspoonfuls of mixture onto wax paper.

- Place in refrigerator for 30 minutes to set. Store in airtight container. Yields 2 dozen.

Tasty Morsel Treats

2 cups butterscotch chips
2 cups salted peanuts
2 cups white raisins

- Mix all ingredients in bowl and store in airtight container. Yields 2 dozen.

A shortcut for homemade cookies is to double the recipe and freeze the extra dough. Roll dough in logs, wrap in plastic wrap or wax paper and seal in a plastic bag. When you're ready to bake, just slice into ¼-inch cookies and bake. It's great to label your package with the name of the cookies, the date frozen, and the cooking temperature and time.

Index

W

Waffles

Water Chestnuts

Y

Z

Zucchini

Cookbooks Published by Cookbook Resources, LLC
Bringing Family and Friends to the Table

The Best 1001 Short, Easy Recipes

1001 Slow Cooker Recipes

1001 Short, Easy, Inexpensive Recipes

1001 Fast Easy Recipes

1001 Community Recipes

Easy Slow Cooker Cookbook

Busy Woman's Slow Cooker Recipes

Busy Woman's Quick & Easy Recipes

Easy Diabetic Recipes

365 Easy Soups and Stews

365 Easy Chicken Recipes

365 Easy One-Dish Recipes

365 Easy Soup Recipes

365 Easy Vegetarian Recipes

365 Easy Casserole Recipes

365 Easy Pasta Recipes

365 Easy Slow Cooker Recipes

Leaving Home Cookbook
and Survival Guide

Essential 3-4-5 Ingredient Recipes

Ultimate 4 Ingredient Cookbook

Easy Cooking with 5 Ingredients

The Best of Cooking with 3 Ingredients

4-Ingredient Recipes for 30-Minute Meals

Cooking with Beer

The Pennsylvania Cookbook

The California Cookbook

Best-Loved New England Recipes

Best-Loved Canadian Recipes

Best-Loved Recipes
from the Pacific Northwest

Easy Slow Cooker Recipes (with Photos)

Cool Smoothies (with Photos)

Easy Cupcakes (with Photos)

Easy Soup Recipes (with Photos)

Classic Tex-Mex and Texas Cooking

Best-Loved Southern Recipes

Classic Southwest Cooking

Miss Sadie's Southern Cooking

Classic Pennsylvania Dutch Cooking

Healthy Cooking with 4 Ingredients

Trophy Hunters' Wild Game Cookbook

Recipe Keeper

Simple Old-Fashioned Baking

Quick Fixes with Cake Mixes

Kitchen Keepsakes &
More Kitchen Keepsakes

Cookbook 25 Years

Texas Longhorn Cookbook

Gifts for the Cookie Jar

All New Gifts for the Cookie Jar

The Big Bake Sale Cookbook

Easy One-Dish Meals

Easy Potluck Recipes

Easy Casseroles

Easy Desserts

Sunday Night Suppers

Easy Church Suppers

365 Easy Meals

Gourmet Cooking with 5 Ingredients

Muffins In A Jar

A Little Taste of Texas

A Little Taste of Texas II

cookbook
resources LLC

www.cookbookresources.com
Your Ultimate Source for Easy Cookbooks

cookbook
resources® LLC

www.cookbookresources.com
Your Ultimate Source for Easy Cookbooks